Timesaver Plays
12 short plays for the classroom

About the book

This book contains 12 short intermediate-level photocopiable plays for the EFL classroom.

Most of the plays contain characters who are near in age (14–16 years old) to the students using the book, and the situations are those with which, in the main, they will be familiar (relationships, friends, parents, etc.).

Each short play ends with a moral dilemma and there are a number of possible solutions which students need to assess, evaluate and discuss.

The accompanying worksheets provide:

- a comprehension check so that students can make sure they have understood the important events in each play.

- a selection of different endings which means that students can think about the problem(s) posed by the play, assess the possible solutions, make value judgements, and then choose the way they themselves would like to see the play actually end.

- a set of language activities reinforcing lexis and grammar.

CONTENTS

Each unit contains a play, a *Comprehension Check*, a *'What Happens Next?'* section and two *Language Practice Worksheets*.

1 The Exam

Characters

Write your name next to the character that you play.

Three school friends:

Maria (girl) _____

Kelly (girl) _____

Adam (boy) _____

Tom (Kelly's boyfriend) _____

Teacher (male or female) _____

Other students (non-speaking) _____

Scene 1: Outside the school gates.

Kelly runs after Adam and Maria.

Kelly: Hey, Maria! Adam! Wait for me!

Adam: Hi, Kelly!
Maria: Hi, Kelly!

Adam: How are things?

Kelly: Great!

Maria: Did you do anything interesting at the weekend?

Kelly: Tom and I went to that new club, *Ego*.

Adam: What's it like?

Kelly: It's fantastic. They've got a brilliant DJ. We danced all night.

Maria: Kelly, you haven't forgotten about tonight, have you?

Kelly: Uh ... I ... er ...

Maria: Kelly! We're going to revise for the chemistry exam. We arranged it last week. Don't you remember?

Kelly: Oh, I'm so sorry, Maria. I forgot! I'm going out with Tom this evening. But we can do our chemistry revision next week, OK? We've got three weeks before the exam.

Maria: Well ... all right. But I really need some help.

Adam: I'd love to help, but I dropped chemistry last year. I've forgotten everything.

Kelly: Chemistry's not my best subject either. I'm not sure if I'll be much help.

Maria: Two heads are better than one! And you <u>did</u> promise ... But I suppose you're right. We've still got time.

Kelly: Oh, there's Anna. I promised to lend her a CD. I've got to go. See you later.

Maria: OK. Bye.

Kelly leaves.

Maria: Adam, I'm really worried about Kelly.

Adam: Why, what's the matter?

Maria: We used to be best friends but since she started going out with Tom, I don't see her much anymore. She's only interested in Tom.

Adam: Don't you like him?

Maria: Well ... no. He's having a bad effect on Kelly's schoolwork. She used to be top in everything. I know she hasn't been doing her homework recently.

Adam: There's still a bit of time before the exams.

Maria: But I know she's not doing any revision, Adam. She's not interested in revision. She doesn't think about anything else except Tom.

Scene 2: Two weeks later in the school corridor during a break in lessons.

Maria bumps into Tom and Kelly.

Maria: Oh hello, Kelly! Hi, Tom!

Tom: Hi, Maria. I haven't seen you for ages.

Kelly: Maria, sorry I haven't helped you with your revision yet, but I've been really busy.

Maria: Don't worry. What about tonight?

Kelly: Oh, sorry, Tom and I are going to the cinema tonight.

Maria: Tomorrow?

Kelly: I promised to help my mum. Actually, Maria, I'm late for a drama lesson. I've got to go.

Maria: It's OK, I understand.

Kelly: Sorry, Maria. I'll call you at home.

Kelly leaves.

Maria: Yeah. Bye, Kelly.

Tom: Maria?

Maria: What?

Tom: You seem a bit miserable lately. Is there a problem?

Maria: No, I'm not miserable. I'm just worried about Kelly. I think she's going to fail her exams.

Tom: You're joking! Kelly's the best in the whole class.

Maria: Well, she <u>was</u> the best ... before she met you.

Tom: What are you trying to say?

Maria: You know what I'm trying to say, Tom.

Maria walks away.

Scene 3: In the examination hall one week later.

Adam: I'm so scared! I get really nervous before exams.

Tom: Me too.

Kelly arrives, looking pale and serious.

Tom: Hi, Kelly. How are things?

Kelly: I feel terrible.

Tom: Don't worry. You'll be fine. Let's sit next to each other.

Teacher: Silence everyone! You have two hours to complete this history exam. No cheating. You will fail the exam if you are caught cheating. Is everyone ready? You may begin.

Tom: *(to himself)* Right. Let's look at the questions. I can answer the first question. And this one! What a relief.

Scene 4: In the examination hall, an hour later.

Teacher: You've got half an hour left.

Tom: *(to himself)* Right, last question.

Tom: What's that noise?

Kelly is getting up, putting on her coat and walking out.

Tom: *(to himself)* What? Kelly's leaving already? I don't think she's finished her paper. Maybe she's ill! I'll just lean over a bit like this so I can see how much she's written.

Tom leans to one side and reads what she has written.

Tom: *(to himself)* I don't believe it! Kelly's answers are exactly the same as mine! She's used exactly the same words! What's she been doing? Has she been copying from me? What are the teachers going to think?

Maria looks across and sees Tom reading Maria's exam paper.

Maria: *(to herself)* I knew it! Tom's cheating. He's copying all his answers from Kelly's paper!

Comprehension check

1. What did Kelly promise Maria?
   ....

2. Why can't Kelly keep her promise to Maria?
   ....

3. How does Kelly try to make Maria feel better about the revision work?
   ....

4. Why can't Adam help Maria?
   ....

5. Why doesn't Maria like Tom?
   ....

6. What does Tom ask Maria?
   ....

7. How does Kelly feel on the first day of the exams?
   ....

8. What does Tom think about the questions on the exam paper?
   ....

9. What does the teacher tell the class about cheating?
   ....

10. What does Maria think when she sees Tom looking at Kelly's paper?
    ....

What happens next?

Read these three suggestions for what happens next.
Explain why they are good ideas or bad ideas. Then choose the way you'd like the play to end.

1

30 minutes later

Teacher: Can you all stop writing, please?

Maria: Mr(s) Fisher, can I have a word with you please?

Teacher: Yes, Maria, what is it?

Maria: Tom's been cheating. He's been copying from Kelly's exam paper.

I think this is a good idea because

....

....

I think this is a bad idea because

....

....

2

Tom: *(to himself)* Oh no! What can I do? I know. I'll change some of my answers. I've got half an hour. I don't want the teachers to think I've been cheating, and I don't want Kelly to get into trouble.

I think this is a good idea because

....

....

I think this is a bad idea because

....

....

3

Maria: *(to herself)* This is really bad! I'm going to tell Kelly about this after the exam.

I think this is a good idea because

....

....

I think this is a bad idea because

....

....

I think the best ending for the play would be

Language Practice Worksheet 1

1 Read the following extracts from the play again.
Underline the best adjective to describe the speaker in each extract.

1. **Kelly:** It's fantastic. They've got a brilliant DJ. We danced all night.
   (tactless / cheerful / untruthful)

2. **Kelly:** But we can do our chemistry revision next week, OK?
   We've got three weeks before the exam.
   (apologetic / angry / upset)

3. **Kelly:** Chemistry's not my best subject either. I'm not sure if I'll be much help.
   (mean / proud / unenthusiastic)

4. **Maria:** But I suppose you're right. We've still got time.
   (reasonable / unreasonable / aggressive)

5. **Maria:** Well, she was the best ... before she met you.
   (ambitious / accusing / friendly)

6. **Tom:** Don't worry. You'll be fine. Let's sit next to each other.
   (humorous / reassuring / happy)

2 All of these sentences are <u>similar</u> to (but not the same as) ones in the play:
Choose the best second half of the conversation each time.

1. Did you do anything interesting on holiday?
   (a) Yes, I've gone to Italy.
   (b) Yes, I'd gone to Italy.
   (c) Yes, I went to Italy.

2. You haven't forgotten about the meeting, have you?
   (a) No, I didn't.
   (b) No, I haven't.
   (c) No, I'm not.

3. What's the matter?
   (a) She wasn't going to school.
   (b) She hadn't been at school.
   (c) She hasn't been going to school.

4. What's she been doing?
   (a) She's looking at my books.
   (b) She'd have looked at my books.
   (c) She's been looking at my books.

5. We discussed it ...
   (a) ... don't you remember?
   (b) ... haven't you remembered?
   (c) ... hadn't you remembered?

6. Hi Sarah. I haven't seen you for a long time.
   (a) I had been really busy.
   (b) I've been really busy.
   (c) I was really busy.

Language Practice Worksheet 2

1 Choose the correct word for each sentence. Put the letters after the words in the correct order and you will discover one of the themes of this play.

cheerful [n]   *angry* [f]   *nervous* [i]   *hungry* [i]   *thirsty* [r]   *beautiful* [s]   *tired* [e]
miserable [d]   *frightening* [h]   *beautiful* [s]   *frightened* [p]

1. I feel .... when someone is rude to me.

2. I get .... when I eat salty food.

3. I often get .... when I've only had a salad for lunch.

4. I feel .... when I have to get up early.

5. A happy book or film always makes me feel ....

6. I feel sorry for my brother because he's unhappy at the moment

   and he always looks so ....

7. Those flowers look so ....

8. Those Halloween masks look very ....

9. I often get .... before a big exam.

10. I feel .... when I read horror stories.

1	2	3	4	5	6	7	8	9	10

2 Which of the following three pictures does <u>not</u> illustrate any of the themes of the play?

2 The Fur Coat

Characters

Write your name next to the character that you play.

Sophie (girl)

_____

Nick (boy, a friend of Sophie's)

_____

Sophie's grandma

_____

Mark (Sophie's brother)

_____

William (boy in Nick's class)

_____

Ella (girl in Sophie's class)

_____

Other students (non-speaking)

_____

Scene 1: In Nick's room at his home.

Sophie: Is everything ready for tomorrow?

Ella: I hope so.

Sophie: I'm really proud of the charity concerts we put on at the youth club.

William: It was a brilliant idea to do this one for *Animals First*.

Sophie: Yes. Lots of people in my class care about animals and animal rights. I'm sure they'll come to the concert.

Ella: What's the matter, Nick? You seem miles away.

Nick: Sorry, I was thinking about my speech. I haven't even started writing it yet.

Sophie: Don't worry, Nick, we'll help you.

William: Yeah. You should say that animals have rights, just like people.

Nick: Hang on. Let me switch on the computer and type in your suggestions.

Ella:	How about 'Meat is murder!'?
Nick:	That's good.
William:	'Fur coats are a crime against nature.'
Sophie:	'... So if you don't eat meat, and you hate fur, please help us to help animals everywhere.'
Nick:	Thanks! It looks like a good speech.
Sophie:	Oh, look at the time! I have to go.
Nick, Ella and Will:	OK, bye.

Scene 2: At Sophie's house.

Sophie:	*(opening the front door)* I'm home!
Mark:	Sophie! We've got a surprise visitor.
Sophie:	Who's that?
Mark:	Look in the kitchen.

Sophie goes to the kitchen.

Sophie:	Gran! How lovely to see you! I didn't know you were coming. How long are you staying?
Gran:	No, I don't think it's raining, dear.
Sophie:	*(shouting louder)* I said 'staying', Gran, not 'raining': How long are you staying?
Gran:	Sorry, I can't hear very well. About a week.
Sophie:	That's really good news.
Gran:	Yes, there are some lovely views from this window, aren't there?
Sophie:	*(shouting)* I said 'good news'!
Gran:	Yes! How are you, Sophie? Are you still enjoying school?
Sophie:	It's brilliant, thanks. We're putting on a big charity concert tomorrow. We want to raise a lot of money.
Gran:	Yes, I'm sure it'll be funny, Sophie. Maybe I can come.
Sophie:	*(shouting)* No, Gran, don't worry, it's not your kind of music ... and anyway, you're deaf – you won't be able to hear. Nick and I are doing it together.
Gran:	Don't worry about the weather. It's only November. No chance of snow.
Sophie:	I didn't say 'weather'; I said 'together'. Nick and I are organising it together.
Gran:	Sorry, dear, what did you say? I'm getting a bit deaf these days.
Sophie:	It doesn't matter ... I love you, Gran! And it would be lovely to see you at the concert. I'll go and get you a ticket from my room.

She hugs her.

Scene 3: In the school hall ... the concert is about to begin; there is excited murmuring from the audience. Nick and Sophie are on stage. William and Ella are on the door, collecting tickets.

Sophie:	Two more minutes before the start, Nick.
Nick:	Are all the musicians ready?
Sophie:	Yes, everyone's backstage. I think you can begin.
Nick:	*(speaks into the microphone)* First of all, th—

A door opens at the back of the hall and everyone looks round. Nick stops halfway through his sentence. Gran enters in a fur coat.

Gran:	Hello!
William:	Can I see your ticket, please?

Gran: *(excitedly)* Here it is. My granddaughter invited me! Isn't that kind of her?

Ella: You can't wear that disgusting fur coat in here!

Gran: No, I haven't got a beer ... can you find her for me?

Sophie: *(to Nick)* I don't believe it! Gran came here wearing a fur coat!

Gran: *(loudly)* Has anyone seen Sophie, my granddaughter? She's organising a concert here at the school.

Some people start giggling and whispering.
Gran walks up the aisle looking at all the faces.

Gran: Sophie! Where are you? I can't see you.

Comprehension check

1. What are Nick and Sophie organising together?

   ....

2. Which charity have they chosen to support this year?

   ....

3. Why is it popular?

   ....

4. Why is Nick worried?

   ....

5. How do Nick's friends help him prepare his speech?

   ....

6. What is Nick going to say about meat?

   ....

7. What is he going to say about wearing fur?

   ....

8. Why doesn't Sophie's gran always understand what people say?

   ....

9. What does Ella think about Sophie's gran's fur coat?

   ....

10. How do the other students react when Sophie's gran is looking for her?

   ....

What happens next?

Read these three suggestions for what happens next.
Explain why they are good ideas or bad ideas. Then choose the way you'd like the play to end.

1

Sophie: Just ignore her, Nick. Go on with your speech. Don't change anything!

Nick: First of all, thank you all for coming. We are here tonight because we want to raise money for *Animals First* ...

I think this is a good idea because

....

....

I think this is a bad idea because

....

....

2

Nick: *(to Sophie)* Oh no! She's ruining everything. There'll be a riot if I try to make my speech.
(loudly) Uh, hello everyone, enjoy the concert.
(to Sophie) Come on, Sophie, let's go backstage. It's a disaster.

I think this is a good idea because

....

....

I think this is a bad idea because

....

....

3

Sophie: *(climbing down from the stage.)* I'm coming, Gran!
You must be so hot in that coat, let me take it for you. I'll take it and put it somewhere safe. You can sit at the back of the hall ... there are some free seats and the music won't be too loud. It's great to see you.

I think this is a good idea because

....

....

I think this is a bad idea because

....

....

I think the best ending for the play would be

Language Practice Worksheet 1

Complete the following sentences using the correct word from each pair.
Put the letter after your chosen word in the correct place in the grid to find a word connected with animal rights.

Sophie's gran is a bit deaf. She can hear but sometimes she gets things wrong.
In English a lot of words sound the same as other words but we spell them differently and you can understand which word belongs in a sentence because of the meaning of the whole sentence.

1. Add some herbs like parsley, garlic and .... to the sauce to make it taste really delicious.

   time [B] / *thyme* [V]

2. May I have a .... of cake, please?

   piece [E] / *peace* [H]

3. She has a .... arm.
   She fell down the stairs and hurt it yesterday.

   saw [A] / *sore* [G]

4. I ran out of the theatre and told my friends
   what I had just ....

   scene [O] / *seen* [E]

5. She jumped into the air and ....
   the ball.

   caught [T] / *court* [B]

6. Guess what I saw in the forest! A ....!

   bare [P] / *bear* [A]

7. I want to .... some skis and go up
   the mountain.

   higher [C] / *hire* [R]

8. On top of the hill, there is a ruin of an old
   Roman ....

   fort [I] / *fought* [E]

9. Nick's speech was difficult to ....

   write [A] / *right* [L]

10. I'm .... with snow-boarding.
    Let's ski now.

    board [L] / *bored* [N]

1	2	3	4	5	6	7	8	9	10

Language Practice Worksheet 2

1 All of these sentences are <u>similar</u> to (but not the same as) ones in the play:
Choose the best second half of the conversation each time.

1. Is everything ready for the show?
   (a) I hope it.
   (b) I think it.
   (c) I hope so.

2. Have you written your speech yet?
   (a) No, I didn't start writing it yet.
   (b) Yes, I wrote it.
   (c) No, I haven't started writing it yet.

3. How long is he staying?
   (a) For two weeks.
   (b) Since two weeks.
   (c) In two weeks' time.

4. Are you enjoying the concert?
   (a) Yes, I enjoy it.
   (b) No, I don't enjoy it.
   (c) Yes, I'm enjoying it.

5. Has anyone seen the play yet?
   (a) No, nobody has seen it yet.
   (b) No, nobody saw it yet
   (c) Yes, we've seen it yet.

2 Add suffixes to change the following words from the play.

Example: brilliant (adjective)   *brilliantly* (adverb)

a. organise (verb) .... (noun)

b. proud (adj) .... (adverb)

c. suggest (verb) .... (noun)

d. nature (noun) .... (adjective)

e. charity (noun) .... (adjective)

f. music (noun) .... (noun, person)

3 Oliver's Diary

Characters

Write your name next to the character that you play.

Three school friends:

Jenny (girl) _____   *Oliver (boy in the same class)* _____

Lily (girl) _____   *Mr Park (their teacher)* _____

Liam (boy) _____

Scene 1: **Early one morning outside the school; Jenny, Lily and Liam are waiting for the bell to ring.**

Lily: Hi, you two! How are things? Have you learned everything for the geography test?

Liam: I'm just hoping that questions about the two topics I prepared come up. If they don't, I'm finished. How about you?

Jenny: I've revised all the topics but I don't think I'll do any better than you, Liam. But Lily's brilliant. She always gets As. She's got a fantastic memory.

Lily: Don't say that! Anyway, let's change the subject. I'm embarrassed. How's the great love of your life, Jenny?

Liam: Love of your life? Who's this, Jenny?

Lily: Go on, Jenny, tell him.

Jenny: Oh, she's teasing me. It's nothing. She knows I like Oliver a lot ...

Liam: Does Oliver know?

Jenny: Of course not! I just adore him from a distance.

The bell rings.

Liam: Oh well, there's the bell.

Lily: Come on, you two! And good luck in the test, everyone!

Scene 2: Early the next day. Jenny and Lily are alone in the classroom.

Jenny: How do you think the test went yesterday?

Lily: It was good. I think I've done well. Hey! What are you doing? That's Oliver's desk!

Jenny: I'm just having a quick look. Maybe he's got some photos of himself in here ...

Lily: Be quick. I'll tell you if anyone is coming.

Jenny opens the desk.

Lily: Have you found anything?

Jenny: No, just the usual ... books, pens ... wait a minute ... what's this right at the back?

Jenny takes a notebook from the desk.

Jenny: Lily, it's a diary.

Lily: It obviously isn't private because he's left it in school.

Jenny: *(reading aloud)* "Tuesday, March the sixth. I have decided to keep my diary in school because I don't want Mum to find it."

Lily: Hey! Let me read. "Wednesday, March the seventh. I managed to speak to Laura for a few minutes yesterday. She's wonderful. She's got such beautiful eyes."

Jenny: I don't believe it! Oliver likes Laura! It's not fair.

Lily: "Wednesday, March the fourteenth. I've spent all my pocket money on two tickets for the Bobby Fillingham

concert on Saturday. Laura is one of his biggest fans. She won't be able to say no. I'll ask her tomorrow."

Jenny: Tomorrow? March the fifteenth ... that's today! He's going to ask her today!

Lily: Look out, Jenny, you've dropped something. Look, there's an envelope on the floor.

Jenny: It's the tickets for the concert!

Lily: Quick, someone's coming. Put everything back.

Mr Park: Hello, Jenny. Hello, Lily. You two are very early for the history lesson. Can't wait to start?

Jenny and Lily: No, sir ..

Jenny: *(to Lily)* Oh no. What am I going to do? I didn't have time to put the tickets back.

Lily: *(to Jenny)* We'll have to wait until the end of the lesson.

Scene 3: In the classroom later during that lesson.

Oliver has got his diary out and is flicking through it.

Lily: *(whispering)* Jenny! What's Oliver doing? I've never seen him with his diary before.

Jenny: Maybe he's looking for the tickets ...

Mr Park: Oliver Grisewood! Give that to me!

Oliver: Excuse me?

Mr Park: Give that to me immediately!

Oliver: But sir, it's my diary.

Mr Park: I don't care. When you are in my lesson you listen to me. You don't read your diary!

Oliver: Please sir! Please don't read it, sir. It's private.

Mr Park: I won't read your diary. But I won't give it back to you until the end of the lesson. Perhaps that will teach you to pay attention in my class.

Jenny: (whispering) Oh, look at Oliver, Lily. Poor thing! He looks so miserable.

At the end of the lesson.

Mr Park: Come to my desk, Grisewood.

Oliver stands up.

Jenny: Mr Park's going to give him his diary back.

Mr Park: I hope you've learned your lesson, Grisewood.

Oliver: Yes, sir.

Oliver rushes back to his desk and starts frantically going through his diary.

Oliver: (to himself) Oh no! They're not here!

Lily: What's the matter, Oliver?

Oliver: I had some tickets for the Bobby Fillingham concert on Saturday. They were in my diary yesterday! Now they've gone!

Lily: I don't know wh...

Oliver: It's Mr Park. He hates me! First he took my diary and now he's stolen my tickets!

Comprehension check

1. Why does Lily tease Jenny?

   ....

2. Does Oliver know how Jenny feels about him?

   ....

3. Why does Jenny look in Oliver's desk?

   ....

4. Why does Lily stand by the classroom door?

   ....

5. What did Oliver buy with his pocket money?

   ....

6. Why didn't Jenny put the tickets back?

   ....

7. What happens to Oliver's diary later in the lesson?

   ....

8. Why is Oliver worried when Mr Park takes his diary?

   ....

9. Why is Oliver upset when he gets his diary back?

   ....

10. What does he think has happened?

   ....

What happens next?

Read these three suggestions for what happens next.
Explain why they are good ideas or bad ideas. Then choose the way you'd like the play to end.

1

Oliver: I'll be back in a minute. I'm going to talk to him about it.

(He goes to talk to Mr Park)

Jenny: Lily, what shall we do?

Lily: Just do nothing. It's too complicated now.

I think this is a good idea because

....

....

I think this is a bad idea because

....

....

2

Jenny: Oliver, listen. Please don't be angry, but I've got the tickets. I found them in your diary. I was looking for a pen in your desk ... anyway, Mr Park came in and I didn't have time to put them back. Here they are.

I think this is a good idea because

....

....

I think this is a bad idea because

....

....

3

Jenny: What's wrong? Can I help?

Oliver: Oh, it doesn't matter. I had some tickets for the Bobby Fillingham concert and now they're gone ...

Jenny: Hey! I've got two tickets for that concert! Do you want to come with me?

I think this is a good idea because

....

....

I think this is a bad idea because

....

....

I think the best ending for the play would be

Language Practice Worksheet 1

All of these things happened in the play, but not in this order. Put the events in the correct order by writing the number of each sentence in the square next to the picture in the story.

1. The concert tickets fell on the floor.

2. Mr Park gave the diary to Oliver.

3. Jenny opened Oliver's desk.

4. Oliver decided to keep his diary in school.

5. Mr Park took Oliver's diary away.

6. Mr Park called Oliver to his desk.

7. Jenny told Liam she liked Oliver.

8. Jenny found Oliver's diary in his desk.

9. Oliver took his diary out of his desk.

Language Practice Worksheet 2

1 Match the sentences halves. Use the two numbers next to the matching sentence halves to join the dots below. They will spell the name of another pop group that was appearing in the concert with Bobby Fillingham.

Oliver will get embarrassed	(1)	☐ (9) if we win the lottery.
Jenny will be happy	(2)	☐ (10) if he passes the test.
You'll be too hot	(3)	1 (11) if Mr Park reads his diary.
We'll be rich	(4)	☐ (12) if I drink some mineral water.
The concert will be cancelled	(5)	☐ (13) if Bobby Fillingham is ill.
I'll feel hungry	(6)	☐ (14) if Oliver asks her out.
Liam will be happy	(7)	☐ (15) if you wear that thick jacket.
Oliver will get fit	(2)	☐ (16) if I don't have breakfast.
Jenny will feel miserable	(9)	☐ (7) if he goes to the gym everyday.
I won't be thirsty	(1)	☐ (17) if Oliver finds out she was looking in his diary.

```
1       12      3       4           17      2       14
●       ●       ●       ●           ●       ●       ●
|
6       16                          5       13
●       ●                          ●       ●
|
11              15          9           7       10
●               ●           ●           ●       ●
```

2 Read Oliver's most recent diary entry. Fill in the gaps with the correct form of the verb in brackets. Use the past simple, past perfect, present continuous for future or present simple.

"Thursday, March the fifteenth. I can't believe what (1) .... (happen) today. First, when I (2) .... (go) into the history class, I immediately (3) .... (open) my desk to look for the concert tickets. I (4) .... (have) to check the time of the concert, before I asked Laura to come. But I (5) .... (not have) time to look for them, because suddenly, Mr Park (6) .... (see) me. I (7) .... (have to give) my diary to him. When he (8) .... (give) it back to me after the lesson, the tickets (9) .... (be) not there. They (10) .... (disappear)! I (11) .... (feel) really upset. Then I (12) .... (discover) that Jenny (13) .... (look) in my desk earlier. I'm not quite sure why ... It's a long story. Anyway, I (14) .... (go) to the concert with Jenny, now. She (15) .... (be) really attractive, and great fun, too. I wonder why I didn't ever notice that before ..."

4 Summer Camp

Characters

Write your name next to the character that you play.

Gemma (girl)

_____

Andy (boyfriend)

_____

Mrs Redwood (Gemma's mum)

_____

Mr Redwood (Gemma's dad)

_____

Richard (injured man)

_____

Susan (injured woman, Richard's wife)

_____

Police officer

_____

Chris Coulson (newspaper journalist)

_____

Scene 1: **In Gemma's house at the start of the summer holidays.**

Mrs Redwood: Gemma, have you packed everything for the camp?

Gemma: *(sighing)* Yes, Mum. I wish you'd stop asking me that!

Mrs Redwood: What about your trainers?

Gemma: I told you! Everything's packed! Anyway, if I forget something, I can buy it in the camp shop.

Mrs Redwood: The camp shop is tiny. They won't sell much there. And it's far away from a supermarket ... in fact, it's far away from anywhere...

Mr Redwood: Well, that's a good thing.

Gemma: What do you mean?

Mr Redwood: You know what I mean, Gemma. You'll be far away from Andy. He's a bad influence on you. Since you met Andy, your behaviour has changed. You're irritable with us; you don't spend enough time on your school work; you go out at night without telling us what time you'll be home...

Gemma: That's not fair! You don't know Andy. He's a good person.

Mr Redwood: Gemma, we don't want you to see him again. Your mother and I have talked about this, and we feel it's the right thing for you – and for Andy. You are both too young to be serious about each other. You've got your future to think about.

Gemma: *(running from the room in tears)* You just don't understand! Leave me alone! I don't want to talk to you!

Scene 2: Later that night at Andy's house.

Andy: Calm down, Gemma. Tell me again what they said. Did they actually say you couldn't ever see me again?

Gemma: Yes. They think it's not going to be a problem because I'm going to summer camp with the youth club tomorrow. The camp is 60 miles away, in the middle of Elsam forest. It's not near a railway station or a bus route ... so we won't be able to see each other for two whole weeks.

Andy: Well, do you want to see me?

Gemma: Of course I do. You know that.

Andy: Well, I've been thinking about this ... and here's my plan. Dad's old motorbike is in the garage. I haven't got a licence because I'm too young, but I can ride a motorbike. I've ridden it before but Dad won't let me ride it without him. It won't take long on a motorbike.

Gemma: But Andy, what will happen if the police catch you ... or if your parents find out?

Andy: Gemma, trust me! I'll be careful. I'll make sure I'm home before they get back from work. When can we meet?

Gemma: Tuesday. I'll have my mobile with me. Ring me when you get to Elsam Forest. I'll meet you at the gate of the camp. Oh Andy! I can't wait!

Andy: Neither can I. I'll miss you! See you on Tuesday.

Gemma: Bye! Take care on the bike!

Scene 3: One week later in Elsam Forest. Andy and Gemma are having a picnic in the forest.

Gemma: What a wonderful day! I'm so glad you came, Andy.

Andy: Me too. Two weeks is too long to be away from each other. Come on, let's go for a walk before you have to go back to the camp.

Gemma: OK. There's a lake near here, just down this path.

There is a terrible crash from the direction of the road.

Gemma: Oh no! What was that noise?

Andy: I don't know ... we'd better find out! Quick! It sounds like a car crash!

They run to the edge of the forest and see that a car has crashed into a tree. The two passengers are screaming.

Woman: Help! Help!

Andy: Gemma, have you got your mobile? Quick! Phone for an ambulance.

Gemma: OK! Andy, they're trapped in the car! Get them out before it catches fire!

Andy: *(to man)* It's OK! I'm going to try to pull you out. Can you move your legs?

Man: I think I've broken my ankle ... and look at all this blood. *(touching his head)* My head's bleeding! Don't worry about me. Help my wife!

Andy: *(to woman)* We'll get you out. What's your name?

Woman: Susan ... and this is my husband, Richard.

Andy: It's OK, Susan. Put your arm round my neck. I'm going to carry you across the grass and I'm going to put my coat round you. Don't move – wait until the ambulance comes ...

Woman: Thank goodness you were here!

Andy: Try to stay quiet ... the ambulance will be here soon.

Gemma: Andy, the ambulance is on its way. Here, take my jumper. Put it under her head.

Andy: Gemma! Run over to the motorbike. There's a small first aid kit in the back! We can do something about Richard's head …

Richard: I don't understand what happened … we've been driving through this forest for years. We've never had an accident before.

Scene 4: **Twenty minutes later. The ambulance is driving away. A police officer and a journalist walk over to Andy and Gemma.**

Police officer: You did a fantastic job. You saved those people's lives.

Andy: Thank you but it was the only thing to do.

Gemma: We just did what was necessary. It was nothing special.

Chris Coulson: *(with camera)* Hi, kids. I'm Chris Coulson. I'm a journalist on the *Elsam Gazette*. You two are heroes. Can I take your photo?

Andy: What?

Chris Coulson: I want to put your photo in the local paper. Now, is that your motorbike over there? Just go and stand next to it. That'll make a great picture.

Gemma: *(whispering)* I'm not allowed to see you! What are we going to do? What will my parents say?

Andy: Yeah! What about my dad? He'll go mad if he finds out I've taken the motorbike!

Comprehension check

1. Why doesn't Mr Redwood like Andy?

....

2. What do Mr and Mrs Redwood think about Gemma's relationship with Andy?

....

3. How far is the camp from Gemma's home?

....

4. What is Andy's plan?

....

5. How are they going to meet?

....

6. Why does Andy try to get Richard and Susan away from the car?

....

7. How do Andy and Gemma try to make the two injured people comfortable?

....

8. Describe the journalist's idea for the perfect photo.

....

9. Why is Gemma worried about the photo in the paper?

....

10. Why is Andy worried about the photo in the paper?

....

What happens next?

Read these three suggestions for what happens next.
Explain why they are good ideas or bad ideas. Then choose the way you'd like the play to end.

1

Chris Coulson: Is something wrong?

Andy: Well, we've got a bit of a problem. You see, that's my dad's bike and he doesn't know I've borrowed it. If he sees my picture in the paper he'll be angry.

Policeman: Do you actually have a licence?

Andy: Uh … no … I …

Policeman: I'm sorry, but I must ask you to come with me to the police station.

I think this is a good idea because

....

....

I think this is a bad idea because

....

....

2

Andy: Oh, I don't care any more. I'm sure Dad won't mind when he learns I'm a hero. Come on, Gemma. Let's do it!

Gemma: I agree! Now they'll really believe me. You're a good person; you're a hero!

I think this is a good idea because

....

....

I think this is a bad idea because

....

....

3

Andy: (to Chris) Please don't be offended, but we're both really shy and we don't think we've done anything special. We don't want any publicity for this.

I think this is a good idea because

....

....

I think this is a bad idea because

....

....

I think the best ending for the play would be

Language Practice Worksheet 1

What's going to happen at Gemma's summer camp tonight?
Find the correct endings to these sentences. They all end with a verb in the future tense.
Put the letters in the correct places in the grid and find the answer.

1. When you arrive at the gate, phone me and

the ambulance will soon be here. [**O**]

2. Don't move! You've broken your ankle;

and everyone will return home. [**Y**]

3. We can meet in secret.

I'll bring a picnic. [**E**]

4. Don't worry about lunch because

he'll take you to the police station and ask you some serious questions. [**A**]

5. Don't worry. When my parents return from work

you'll catch a cold. [**P**]

6. I've just phoned the hospital and

I'll meet you. [**F**]

7. You can phone me because

I think it'll catch fire. [**K**]

8. We must get you away from the car because

he'll go mad. [**T**]

9. If you go out in the rain without a coat

I'll already be home and they won't guess what I've been doing. [**W**]

10. When the policeman discovers you are riding this bike without a licence

I'll get you out. [**I**]

11. My watch has stopped and I don't know the time so

I'll have my mobile with me. [**R**]

12. When my dad finds out I've taken his bike

Nobody will ever know. [**R**]

13. Summer camp finishes at the end of August

I'll probably be late. [**R**]

Tonight there's going to be a

1	2	3	4	5	6	7	8		9	10	11	12	13
☐	☐	☐	☐	☐	☐	☐	☐		☐	☐	☐	☐	☐

Language Practice Worksheet 2

Unjumble the words on the poster to find ten activities at the summer camp.

SUMMER CAMP

COME TO
SUMMER CAMP AND TRY SOMETHING NEW

a. FURINGSWIND

b. GINCONAE

c. MALPINITRONG

d. GLYCINC

e. GASIBLINE

f. TRIGWIN

g. BLEYLOVALL

h. TINPANIG

i. YOPTERT

j. RAMAD

5 The Secret

Characters

Write your name next to the character that you play.

Sarah (girl)

_____

Eddie (boy, Sarah's friend)

_____

Rachel (girl, Sarah's friend)

_____

Doctor Warner

_____

Mrs Philpott (Sarah's mother)

_____

Joel (boy that Sarah fancies)

_____

Scene 1: **Outside the school gates.**

Eddie: Sarah, how about going to the cinema on Saturday?

Sarah: Well, I don't know …

Eddie: Come on. It's *Club Days*, this film about people at a club in New York, with an amazing soundtrack …

Sarah: *(quickly)* Oh, no, I don't want to see that, Eddie, sorry.

Eddie: Really? But you usually love that kind of thing!

Sarah: Well, I used to, but ….

Eddie: OK, let's go to *The Cross* then? That new DJ is going to be there, the one who just made an album in Ibiza …

Sarah: Sorry, Eddie, I don't go to clubs any more.

Eddie: What? Why not? You've never refused to go clubbing before! What's happened to you, Sarah?

Sarah: It's a long story. It's making me really depressed.

Eddie: Sarah, you look so upset … Tell me about it. Come on, sit down …

Scene 2: **At Dr Warner's surgery three weeks earlier.**

Dr Warner: Hello, Sarah, Mrs Philpott. What seems to be the problem?

Mrs Philpott: Sarah, explain exactly what has been happening.

Sarah: Well, for the past three or four months I've been hearing strange noises in my ears and I can't always hear what people are saying when I am in a crowded room.

Dr Warner: Can you describe those noises?

Sarah: It's a kind of ringing … or whistling … it's difficult to explain.

Dr Warner: *(checking Sarah's ears)* Do you listen to loud music a lot, Sarah?

Sarah: Well, yes, I suppose I do … I mean, everyone does …

Dr Warner: I'm afraid we don't really have the right equipment here to do a really thorough hearing test, so I'm going to get you an appointment at Greenwood Hospital. They specialise in hearing tests, so I'm sure we'll find out what the problem is.

Scene 3: Dr Warner's surgery a few weeks later.

Dr Warner: Well, I've got the results of the hospital tests here, Sarah, and I'm afraid it's not very good news.

Sarah: Oh, no …

Mrs Philpott: What have they found, Doctor Warner?

Dr Warner: Well, Sarah's got some hearing loss in both ears. It's impossible to say if it's likely to get worse, but I have to tell you that it is permanent. So, I strongly recommend that you avoid situations where there is loud music or noise, Sarah.

Sarah: *(quietly)* Thank you, Dr Warner. Goodbye.

Dr Warner: Goodbye, Sarah, goodbye, Mrs Philpott.

Scene 4: In the street near the school.

Eddie: Sarah, that's awful news.

Sarah: Yeah.

Eddie: So that's why you don't want to come out with me on Saturday night.

Sarah: That's right. Don't tell anyone else, OK? I'm not ready for that …

Eddie: Of course not. Oh, here's my bus. See you. Any time you need to talk, just call me, OK?

Sarah: Thanks, Eddie.

Rachel gets off the bus.

Rachel: Sarah!

Sarah doesn't hear first time so she calls a little louder.

Rachel: Sarah!

Sarah: Oh, hi, Rachel. How are things?

Rachel: OK. What were you and Eddie talking about?

Sarah: He wanted to go to the cinema on Saturday but I'm not in the mood.

Rachel: Poor Eddie. I think he's in love with you!

Sarah: Don't be silly. Eddie and I are best friends. We could never go out together. It would ruin everything. Now, if Joel wanted to go out on Saturday …

Rachel: Sarah, every girl in the school wishes that!

Sarah: I know. I haven't got a chance with him. Imagine, the lead singer in a band, asking me out! Did you know he writes all the songs for the band? They are so … personal, do you know what I mean? I wonder who he thinks about when he writes them …

Rachel: Sshh! He's just over there. He'll hear you!

Joel: Hi, Rachel. Hi, Sarah.

Rachel and Sarah: Hi.

Joel: Um … Sarah, I've been wanting to talk to you for ages.

Rachel: Oh, I've just remembered something … I've got to go …

Joel: The band's got a gig on Saturday. I'd really like you to come.

Sarah: Me?

Joel: Why do you seem so surprised?

Sarah: Well, I didn't know you … I mean … thanks.

Joel: So you'll come?

Sarah: I … I don't know … I'm not sure. Look, I'd better go, Joel.

Sarah hurries off, head down. Joel looks puzzled and hurt.

Scene 5: Later that day in the café near the school.

Joel: Hi, Eddie.

Eddie: Hi, Joel. How's it going?

Joel: Fine.

Eddie: Well, you don't look too happy. What's up?

Joel: Eddie, you and Sarah are good friends, aren't you?

Eddie: Yes. Why? Did she say anything to you about me?

Joel: No. Why?

Eddie: *(disappointed)* Oh, it's nothing …

Joel: Well, is everything alright with her?

Eddie: What do you mean?.

Joel: I've fancied her for ages, you know.

Eddie: Really? No, I didn't know …

Joel: I asked her to come to our gig on Saturday. She seemed really pleased. But then she sort of … *ran off*. As if she suddenly remembered something. I just wondered what was going on. Do you know?

Comprehension check

1. Why is Eddie excited about *The Cross* on Saturday night?

....

2. Why did Sarah see the doctor?

....

3. How long has Sarah been having this problem with her ears?

....

4. What advice did Dr Warner give Sarah?

....

5. Why doesn't Sarah want Eddie to be her boyfriend?

....

6. Why can't Sarah imagine why Joel would be interested in her?

....

7. What does Joel invite Sarah to?

....

8. Why does Sarah run off without answering Joel's question?

....

9. Why is Eddie disappointed that Sarah hasn't said anything to Joel about him?

....

10. Why does Joel ask Eddie's advice about Sarah?

....

What happens next?

Read these three suggestions for what happens next.
Explain why they are good ideas or bad ideas. Then choose the way you'd like the play to end.

1

Eddie: It's a bit sensitive, Joel … and it's a secret. Sarah doesn't want people to know this, but I'll tell you, because I know you like her. She's going deaf. She has a problem with her hearing and she can't go anywhere where there is a lot of noise.

Next day at school.

Joel: Hi, Sarah. Listen, Eddie told me about your problem …

I think this is a good idea because

....
....
....
....

I think this is a bad idea because

....
....
....
....

2

Eddie: I can't really discuss it. I'm sure Sarah will explain it to you when she's ready.

Next day at school.

Joel: Hi, Sarah.

Sarah: Hi Joel. I'm sorry about yesterday. It's a bit embarrassing but I've got quite a serious problem with my hearing. I can't go to places where there's a lot of noise. Perhaps we can meet another time … go for a pizza … a walk or something?

Joel: Right. Um … Sure. I'll call you. It's going to be difficult though, this term … the band's got a lot of gigs on ….

I think this is a good idea because

....
....
....

I think this is a bad idea because

....
....
....
....

3

Eddie: As far as I know there isn't a problem. Don't worry.

Next day at school.

Joel: Hi, Sarah.

Sarah: Hi, Joel. I'd love to come on Saturday. What time is the gig?

I think this is a good idea because

....
....
....

I think this is a bad idea because

....
....
....
....

I think the best ending for the play would be

Language Practice Worksheet 1

**What's the name of Joel's band? Answer the questions in the maze
and write the letters of all the correct answers as you go through it.**

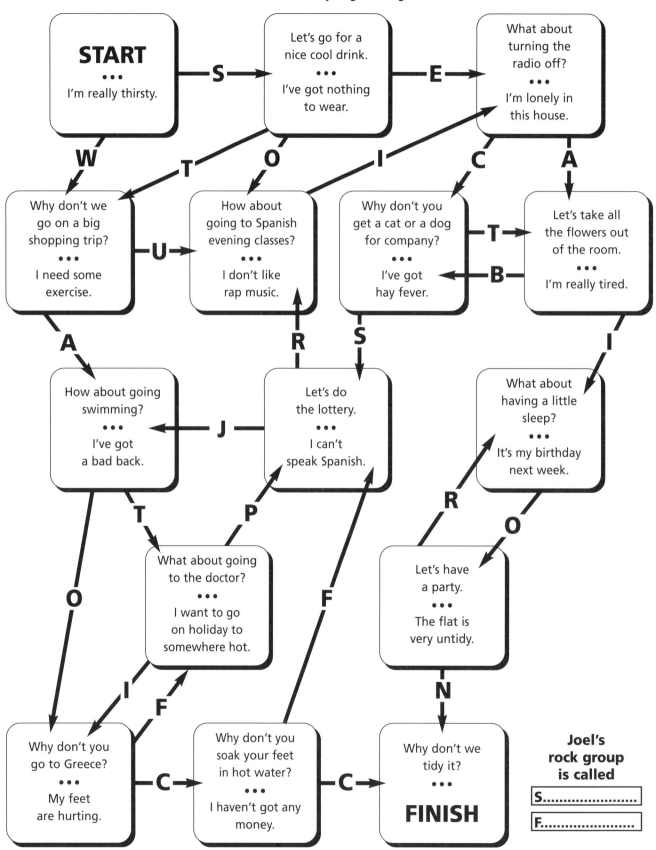

START
...
I'm really thirsty.

S →

Let's go for a
nice cool drink.
...
I've got nothing
to wear.

E →

What about
turning the
radio off?
...
I'm lonely in
this house.

W

T

O

I

C

A

Why don't we
go on a big
shopping trip?
...
I need some
exercise.

U →

How about
going to Spanish
evening classes?
...
I don't like
rap music.

Why don't you
get a cat or a dog
for company?
...
I've got
hay fever.

T →
B

Let's take all
the flowers out
of the room.
...
I'm really tired.

A

R

S

I

How about going
swimming?
...
I've got
a bad back.

J

Let's do
the lottery.
...
I can't
speak Spanish.

What about
having a little
sleep?
...
It's my birthday
next week.

T

P

F

R

O

O

What about going
to the doctor?
...
I want to go
on holiday to
somewhere hot.

Let's have
a party.
...
The flat is
very untidy.

N

I

F

Why don't you
go to Greece?
...
My feet
are hurting.

C →

Why don't you
soak your feet
in hot water?
...
I haven't got any
money.

C →

Why don't we
tidy it?
...
FINISH

**Joel's
rock group
is called**

S.....................

F.....................

Language Practice Worksheet 2

1 Read these sentences from the play. Then choose the sentence (a – c) that contains the most accurate explanation of each sentence.

1. I've been hearing strange noises in my ears.
   (a) I don't hear them anymore.
   (b) I'm still hearing them.
   (c) I heard strange noises once before.

2. You've never refused to go clubbing!
   (a) This is the first time you've refused to go clubbing.
   (b) You aren't refusing to go clubbing.
   (c) Please don't refuse to go clubbing.

3. It's making me really depressed.
   (a) I don't feel very happy.
   (b) I didn't feel very happy.
   (c) I'm going to be very unhappy.

4. I've been wanting to talk to you for ages.
   (a) I still want to talk to you.
   (b) I wanted to talk to you once before.
   (c) I talked to you a few minutes ago.

5. The band's got a gig on Saturday.
   (a) We're playing every Saturday night.
   (b) We usually play on Saturday nights.
   (c) We're going to play on Saturday night.

2 Find words in List B which can have the opposite meaning to the words from the play in List A.

A
awful
crowded
permanent
strange
thorough
upset
worried

B
carefree
empty
familiar
quick
calm
temporary
wonderful

6 The Charity Box

Characters

Write your name next to the character that you play.

Sam (boy) _____

Tessa (girl, Sam's girlfriend)

_____

Tracey (girl) _____

Ricky (boy) _____

Tim (boy) _____

Harriet (girl) _____

Holly (girl) _____

Liz (girl) _____

Scene 1: December 21st, at Tracey's Christmas party.

Music, lots of young people dancing; the sound of the doorbell.

Tim: Tracey!

Ricky: Tracey! Doorbell!

Tracey opens the door

Tracey: Harriet! Nice to see you.

Harriet: Thanks for inviting me, Tracey.

Tracey: Well, it'll be a good way for you to meet people from the neighbourhood. How are you settling in?

Harriet: Oh, it's great. Everyone's really friendly. Who's that guy that just came in, by the way?

Tracey: Who? Oh, Sam! Don't get too keen on him! He's just started going out with a girl in my class called Tessa.

Harriet: Oh, what a pity!

Tracey: Yes, he's gorgeous, isn't he? It's funny, he's not really Tessa's type at all.

Harriet: What's she like, then?

Tracey: She's really serious. She's involved with *Save the Children* projects, and the *Young Green Party*, things like that. But Sam is crazy about her. I'll introduce you to him. Come on. Sam! Hi! Welcome to the party. I'm so pleased you've come.

Sam: Hi, Tracey.

Tracey: This is Harriet. She's new to the area.

Sam: Hi, Harriet. Pleased to meet you.

Harriet: Pleased to meet you, Sam.

Ricky: Sam! What's it like to be a millionaire?

Tim: How did you get some time off from work?

Harriet: Where are you working, Sam?

Sam: I've been working three evenings a week at the petrol station.

Harriet: Three evenings a week? That's a lot!

Tim: And he's been rehearsing for the school musical! Are you saving up for something, Sam?

Ricky: Yeah, we all want to see what you're going to spend your fortune on, Sam!

Sam laughs nervously and walks away.

Tracey: Is everything alright, Sam?

Sam: Yeah. I'm just tired, that's all.

Tracey: It's because you've been working so hard, Sam. Where's Tessa tonight?

Sam: Oh, she's collecting money for charity. She'll be here later. It's late-night shopping in the town centre and then they're going round some of the expensive boutiques in the area.

Tracey: She's really committed, isn't she?

Sam: Yes, she's been working so hard at raising money for charity this year – she never spends any money on herself, you know – she's too conscious of the fact that so many people are suffering from poverty in the world. That's why I've been working so hard at the petrol station. I decided to get her something really special for Christmas. It's a Luc Charpentier jacket.

Tracey: Sam! Luc Charpentier stuff costs a fortune. Kate Moss wears Charpentier all the time. It's going to be outrageously expensive. Are you sure you've got enough money?

Sam: I've already bought it! I just went home to drop it off and came straight here. I've finished working at the petrol station now. I've just got enough money for the bus fare home tonight – and that's it!

Tracey: Sam, Tessa's going to love it. She must be the luckiest girl in the world to have a boyfriend like you!

Scene 2: **At the party a few hours later. Tessa and a few of her friends arrive carrying collecting boxes.**

Tessa: Hi, everyone! Hi Sam!

She squeezes his arm.

Sam: Hi, Tess. Had a good evening?

Tessa: Absolutely brilliant. We've collected lots of money, didn't we, girls?

Holly: It was amazing.

Liz: Yes. My box is really heavy. I can't wait to know how much we collected.

Tessa: I can't believe it. You know, some people are so generous and others are so mean. They're happy to throw their money around for expensive Christmas presents but when it comes to giving it to charity …

Tracey: But it's nice to be able to buy people presents, don't you think?

Tessa: Sure, I like giving presents, and getting them, of course, but I find it really disgusting when people spend a fortune on things like designer clothes. You can get the same thing at second hand shops!

Holly: Come on, we still haven't collected enough. So we've decided to have a big collection here at the party. You'll all give us something, won't you?

Liz: It's for an excellent cause. There are kids in Africa who are very poor. They'll die without your money. Come on, who's going to give us some money?

Tessa: Sam! You've got lots of money! You must be the richest boy in the room! You've been working at the petrol station for weeks. Let's start with you.

Sam: Uh … I …

Comprehension check

1. Who is giving the party?

....

2. Why doesn't Harriet know many people in the neighbourhood?

....

3. Why does Tracey think Sam isn't Tessa's type?

....

4. Where has Sam been working for the last three weeks?

....

5. Why didn't Tessa come to the party with Sam?

....

6. Where are Tessa and her friends collecting money?

....

7. Why doesn't Tessa spend much money on herself?

....

8. Why has Sam been working so hard?

....

9. What does Tracey think of Sam's present?

....

10. Why is it a problem for Sam to give money to the charity?

....

What happens next?

Read these three suggestions for what happens next.
Explain why they are good ideas or bad ideas. Then choose the way you'd like the play to end.

1

Tessa: What's the problem?

Sam: Can I talk to you alone for a moment?

Tessa: OK. Hang on, everybody. I'll be back in a minute. Get your money ready!

I think this is a good idea because

....

....

I think this is a bad idea because

....

....

2

Tracey: OK everyone, let's dance! Tim! Turn up the volume! Come on, Sam, let's dance!

Tessa: *(to herself)* I don't believe it. He's trying to get out of putting in money! What kind of person is he?

I think this is a good idea because

....

....

I think this is a bad idea because

....

....

3

Tracey: Tessa, maybe it's better if we all give you the money tomorrow.
Some people haven't got their wallets or purses with them.
I'm sure you can wait a few more hours.

I think this is a good idea because

....

....

I think this is a bad idea because

....

....

I think the best ending for the play would be ⟨　　　　⟩

Language Practice Worksheet 1

Sam is writing his diary. Choose the correct verbs and write the letters in the grid. You can find out what the charity is going to buy with the money which Tessa and her friends have collected.

Tonight I .... (1) (went **B** / have gone **E**) to Tracey's house

because she .... (2) (had given **B** / was giving **L**) a party.

I .... (3) (was getting **H** / got **A**) a drink and ....

(4) (was going **P** / went **N**) into the sitting room. People ....

(5) (have made **C** / were making **K**) jokes about my job – because they think I

.... (6) (was earning **A** / have earned **E**) lots of money. In fact,

I almost .... (7) (have fallen **W** / fell **T**) asleep on my feet

because I was so tired. Tessa wasn't there because she .... (8)

(collected **R** / was collecting **S**) money for charity. After .... (9)

(to collect **W** / collecting **M**) money in the town centre, Tessa

.... (10) (has gone **N** / went **E**) onto the boutiques in the area

and so she .... (11) (was going to arrive **D** / has been arriving **M**)

late. I .... (12) (had told **I** / have told **U**) Tracey about the

Charpentier jacket I had bought for Tessa. Tessa and her friends

.... (13) (have come **L** / came **C**) through the door a few hours

later. Liz .... (14) (said **I** / has said **D**) her box

.... (15) (had felt **T** / felt **N**) really heavy. Then, to my horror,

they .... (16) (were deciding **I** / decided **E**) to have another

collection at the party.

Answer:

and

Language Practice Worksheet 2

Read the clues and find the words in the play. Write the words in the grid.
The shaded squares will spell the word for someone with a huge amount of money.

1. The school performance that Sam was rehearsing for.
2. This word describes expensive clothes with famous labels.
3. Tracey describes Tessa as the _____ (most fortunate) girl in the world.
4. The place where Sam has been working.
5. To arrange for two people to meet for the first time.
6. To be dedicated to something.
7. This word describes someone who gives freely and selflessly.
8. An organisation which raises money for worthy causes.
9. The local area.
10. *Poor* is the adjective. What is the noun?
11. Not lighthearted or silly.

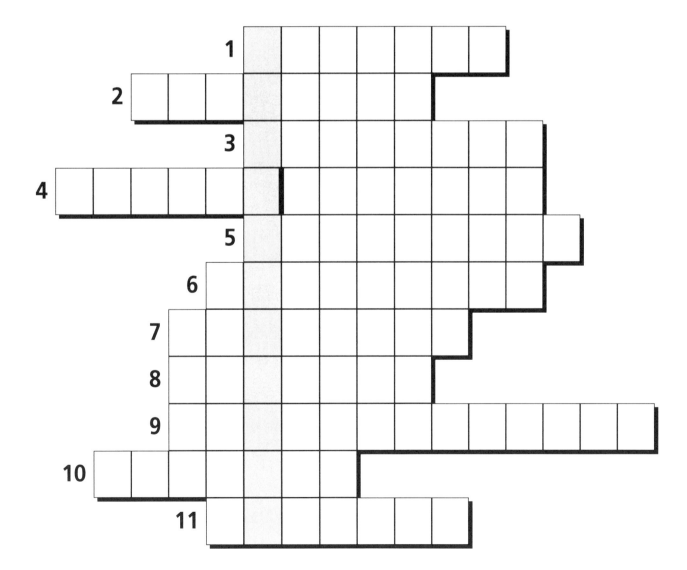

7 The Joke

Characters

Write your name next to the character that you play.

Anna (girl)

_____

Matthew (boy, Anna's brother)

_____

Patrick (boy, Anna and Matthew's cousin)

_____

Anna and Matthew's mum

_____

Scene 1: **A big old house in the country. Anna and her cousin, Patrick, are sitting on the verandah in the evening.**

Anna: What a beautiful evening! I really love spending the holidays here with you and Uncle Roland. You're so lucky to live here all the year. It's paradise.

Patrick: Yes, the countryside's really lovely in the summer.

Anna: What are those little birds? Surely it's too late to see birds.

Patrick: They're not birds, Anna. They're bats! You city kids don't often see them, do you? When's Matt coming home?

Anna: Oh, soon, I think. Oh, look, he's coming down the lane on his bike.

Matthew: Hi, you two. What are you doing?

Anna: We're just enjoying the evening out here on the verandah. We've just seen some bats.

Matthew: Bats! They remind me of ghosts.

Patrick: Do you know that there's a ghost in this house?

Anna: You're joking!

Patrick: No, I mean it. He comes every year on July the thirteenth, in the evening, just before eight o'clock. He's always in white and he wears a chef's hat. He was probably a cook who lived in the house long ago. He comes back once a year to serve his final meal.

Matthew: You don't really believe in ghosts, do you, Anna?

Anna: You're always playing jokes, Patrick. You're teasing me, right?

Patrick: I'm only telling you what I've heard, Anna.

Anna: But today's the thirteenth of July! Is that why you're telling us this story?

Patrick: Well, yes, I just didn't want you to be frightened, that's all. You see – I'm sorry about this – dad has to go out to a meeting in the village. And I'm going out with my girlfriend tonight. That's why I'm glad Matthew is here to keep you company, Anna – especially tonight …

Anna: Oh, stop it, Patrick. Matthew, you're not going out, I hope.

Matthew: No, I'll stay here and keep the ghosts away.

Anna: Let's just forget about that story, please ...

Scene 2: About an hour later.

Patrick: Well, I've got to go. Enjoy yourselves!

Matthew: Bye! Come on, Anna. Let's go and choose a video for later.

Anna: You go ahead. I'll get a drink from the kitchen.

Scene 3: In the sitting room.

Anna: Matthew? Matthew! Where are you?

The door opens and Matthew enters with a towel on his head, acting like a ghost.

Matthew: Whoooo!

Anna: Matthew! Take that towel off your head and behave yourself. Come on, let's find a video. I don't want a scary film tonight. I just want some gentle entertainment. What's the time now?

Matthew: Seven fifteen.

Anna: I promised to phone Mum this evening. I'll do that now, then I'll go and make supper.

Scene 4: Anna on the phone to her mum.

Anna: Hello, mum.

Anna's mum: Hello, darling! How are you? Are you having a good time?

Anna: Oh, it's been great here. We've been swimming in the river, and riding our mountain bikes in the forest ...

Anna's mum: You won't want to come back to city life!

Anna: Well, I don't know ... mum, do you know anything about a ghost that comes here at the end of every summer?

Anna's mum: What's Patrick been telling you now?

Anna: Did you ever see a ghost when you were a little girl here? In a chef's hat?

Anna's mum: Oh, that's just a silly story. Don't take it seriously. You know what Patrick's like. He's always playing tricks on people and trying to frighten them. Although, Grandpa used to tell us the same story ...

Anna: What! It's obviously true, then! I thought Patrick was just making it up!

Anna's mum: It's just a story, Anna, that's all. Maybe there's some truth in it, I don't know. I certainly haven't seen this ghost, and I lived in that house for years! Now, tell me, how's Matthew?

Scene 5: Anna is alone in the kitchen, quarter of an hour later, looking through a recipe book.

Anna: Now what am I going to cook? Pancakes ... with chicken and spinach ... that sounds nice. So, I need flour, *(opens cupboard)* ... here we are, and milk *(opens fridge)* and an egg. Spinach – oh, good, he's got some. Now where's the salt? That's funny ... *(to herself)* It's usually here on this shelf.

Anna: *(opening small cupboards)* No ... not here ... nor here ...

Anna: I've looked everywhere ... maybe it's in this big cupboard.

As she opens the cupboard Matthew jumps out.

Matthew: Whooo!

Anna: Aaagghhh!

She screams and jumps backwards straight against the kitchen table. Expensive glasses and plates fall to the floor and smash.

Anna: You idiot! That's really stupid! Look what you've made me do! Get out! Just go away!

Matthew makes a quick exit.

Anna: Oh no, it's five to eight! I'm not going to stay here on my own. What am I going to do?

Scene 6: In the garden near the garden shed.

Voice in shed: Ha! Ha! Ha!

Matthew: Who's that?

Matthew stands on his toes and looks through the window.

Matthew: Oh no! It's Patrick, dressed up in a chef's hat and a white sheet! He's going to play a trick on us! Patrick! I thought you were going out tonight!

Patrick: Oh, I just made up that story. I want to scare Anna! She really believed me when I told her that story about the ghost!

Matthew: Don't scare Anna, please. She's really terrified. I was just messing about and she went crazy! We'd better go back inside with her.

Patrick: Oh, Matthew, don't be such a spoilsport! Honestly, you're not much fun, are you? Stop being so sensible all the time! Come on, it'll be a laugh!

Comprehension check

1. What are Patrick and Anna doing in the evening?
....

2. What does Anna see in the sky?
....

3. Why does Matthew mention ghosts?
....

4. At what time and on which day of the year does the ghost visit the house?
....

5. What does the ghost look like?
....

6. On which day does the story take place?
....

7. Why are Anna and Matthew going to be alone in the house later?
....

8. Why does Anna ask her mum about the ghost story?
....

9. What is Patrick doing in the shed?
....

10. Why does Matthew feel they should go back and stay with Anna?
....

What happens next?

Read these three suggestions for what happens next.
Explain why they are good ideas or bad ideas. Then choose the way you'd like the play to end.

1

Matthew: No, Patrick. It's a cruel trick to play on her. You know she's a sensitive person. She really is afraid. I don't care if you think I'm a spoilsport. I think you're really childish!

I think this is a good idea because

....

....

I think this is a bad idea because

....

....

2

Matthew: Well … OK! You're right. Put the sheet over me as well, then we'll look really huge! Let's creep into the kitchen and make ghostly noises!

I think this is a good idea because

....

....

I think this is a bad idea because

....

....

3

Matthew: Well … you can try and scare her, then, if you want to, but I'm not going to.
Patrick: Don't tell her it's me, OK?
Matthew: I won't tell her, don't worry …

I think this is a good idea because

....

....

I think this is a bad idea because

....

....

I think the best ending for the play would be ⟨　　⟩

Language Practice Worksheet 1

Match the types of video and the video covers.
The cover left over is the video Anna chooses to watch.

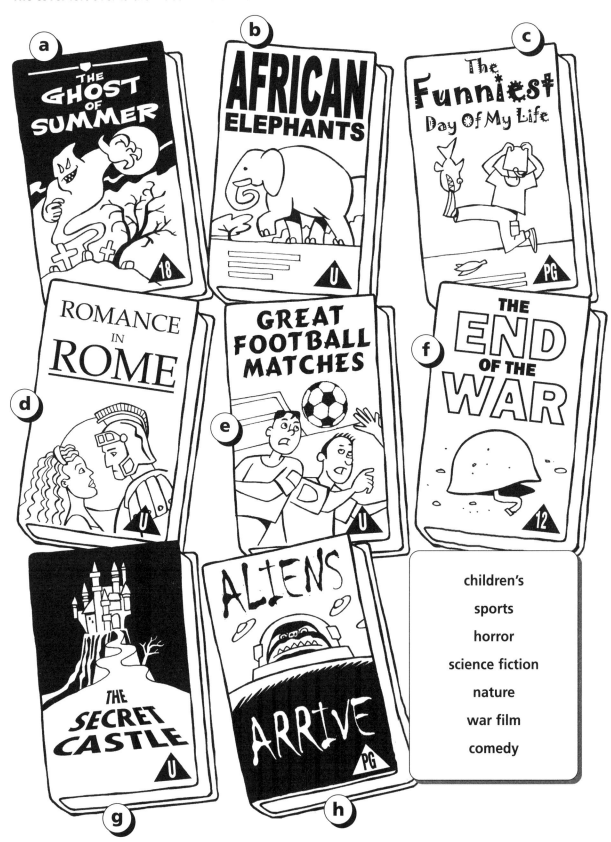

a THE GHOST OF SUMMER 18

b AFRICAN ELEPHANTS U

c The Funniest Day Of My Life PG

d ROMANCE IN ROME U

e GREAT FOOTBALL MATCHES U

f THE END OF THE WAR 12

g THE SECRET CASTLE U

h ALIENS ARRIVE PG

children's

sports

horror

science fiction

nature

war film

comedy

Language Practice Worksheet 2

Complete the crossword with words from the play.

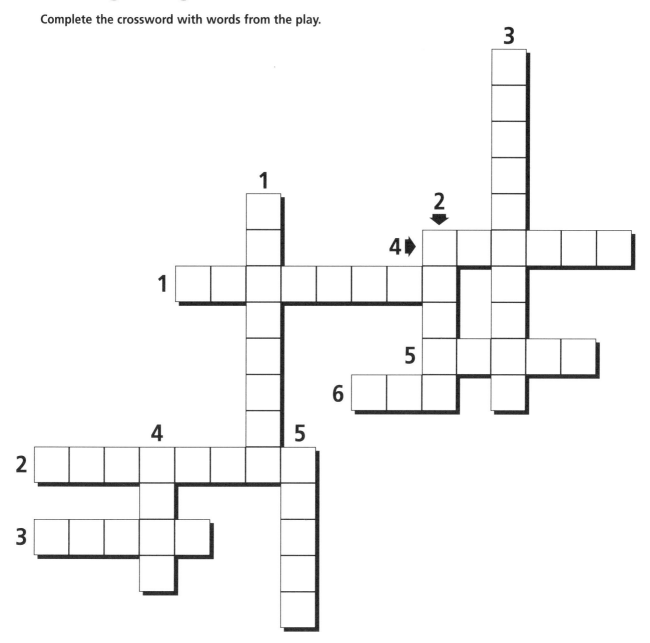

Across

1. The area outside the house where Anna and Patrick were sitting in the evening

2. The supper Anna was preparing

3. The object Matthew put over his head to scare Anna

4. The kind of film Anna wanted to watch

5. The object Patrick covered himself in, to pretend to be a ghost

6. The flying creatures Anna saw in the garden

Down

1. The word Anna used to describe the house and the garden in the evening

2. The 'person' that appeared every year on July the thirteenth

3. The place where Patrick was hiding (2 words)

4. The job the ghost once had

5. The kind of film that makes you frightened

8 Friendship and Lies

Characters

Write your name next to the character that you play.

Lia (girl)

_____

Rory (Lia's boyfriend)

_____

Donna (girl, Lia's friend)

_____

Claire (girl, Lia's cousin)

_____

Shop assistant

_____

Mr Snowdon (Donna's father)

_____

Scene 1: Outside the school.

Rory: But Lia, it's Friday night. You can't do homework on a Friday night! Everyone goes out on Friday night ... and you're supposed to be my girlfriend!

Lia: Sorry, Rory. You know how strict my dad is. I have to revise for my exams.

Rory: Well, you've got to make your choice – it's either me or schoolwork. What's the point of us going out with each other, if we never actually go anywhere together?

Lia: It's only because I've got exams soon – I'm not always studying!

Rory: You should try and have more fun, ☞ Lia. Your friends go out, and they pass their exams! Why can't you be more like Donna, for example? Now that's what I call a fun person ...

Lia: Donna's not trying to get into university, like I am. I'm not going to let you or anyone else spoil my chances of a great future. Why can't we meet up in town on Saturday instead?

Rory: You know I always play basketball on Saturday mornings. Anyway, Friday night's the night for going out!

Lia: You're being really childish, Rory. I'm going home now. See you.

Scene 2: **The next morning; Lia is in a large clothes shop with her cousin, Claire.**

Lia: It's a pity Rory couldn't come into town today.

Claire: Rory doesn't enjoy shopping though. We'll have lots of fun. How about this T-shirt?

Lia: I can't wear a T-shirt saying 'School stinks'! Dad would kill me!

Donna and Rory come into the shop. They can't see Lia as she is behind a rail of jeans.

Lia: There's Rory! He said he was playing basketball.

Claire: Where?

Lia: Over there! He's looking at those T-shirts we just saw.

Claire: Is that the boy you told me about? Who's the girl he's with?

Lia: I don't believe it! It's Donna! She's my best friend … what's she doing with Rory? Quick, let's hide in this changing room. I don't want them to see me.

Donna: I've got an idea. Go outside for a minute, Rory. I want to buy you something.

Rory: A present? OK. Don't be long.

Lia: What's she going to do?

Claire: Open the door a little bit. We'll be able to see from here.

Shop assistant: Can I help you?

Donna: Yes, can I see those earrings, please, those little silver ones in the cabinet?

Shop assistant: I'll just go and get the key.

The shop assistant disappears. Donna steals two T-shirts and puts them into her bag quickly.

Lia: I don't believe it! Donna's shoplifting! She just put those T-shirts into her bag! I've been friends with Donna for years and I never knew she was a thief.

The shop assistant returns with earrings.

Shop assistant: Would you like to try them on?

Donna: Actually, they aren't quite what I expected. No, thank you, I won't take them.

Donna leaves the shop.

Shop assistant: *(to Lia)* How are the jeans? Any luck?

Lia: I'm afraid not. They're not the right style. They're too baggy.

Shop assistant: OK. No problem.

Scene 3: **In the street outside the shop a few minutes later.**

Claire: Let's go and have some coffee, Lia. You look pretty shaken.

Lia: Yes, I am. First seeing Rory and Donna together … and then seeing Donna shoplifting like that! I can't believe it …

Claire: Look, that policeman's talking to the shop assistant who served you …

Scene 4: **That afternoon: in the park. Rory is wearing a T-shirt with the words: 'School stinks!' on it.**

Donna: Lia! Lia! Come and sit over here with me and Rory!

Lia: Hi, Rory. Hi, Donna. What a surprise. Rory, don't you usually play basketball on Saturday mornings?

Rory: Yes, usually, but I decided to enjoy the good weather instead. Donna and I have just been relaxing here in the park.

Lia: Oh … Donna, isn't that your dad? He's coming over here.

Donna: Hi, Dad!

Mr Snowdon: Donna! At last I've found you. I've been looking for you everywhere. You left your purse at home this morning with all your money in it. And where did you get that awful T-shirt? I see you've got one too, Rory.

Rory: Yes, it was a present, actually, from … wait a minute, *(to Donna)* how did you …

Mr Snowdon: Well, I'm glad it wasn't a present from you, Donna! I really don't like it.

Donna: No, Dad, of course it wasn't from me. It was from Lia.

Rory: What? But you said …

Mr Snowdon: Lia gave you each a T-shirt saying 'School stinks!'? I don't believe it! Lia, you're the head girl, the top student! This isn't like you at all! What were you thinking?

Comprehension check

1. What are Rory and Lia arguing about?

....

2. Why does Lia want to do revision on a Friday night?

....

3. What does Rory think about her attitude towards her schoolwork?

....

4. How does Lia describe Rory's behaviour?

....

5. What does Lia suggest doing instead of going out on Friday night?

....

6. What two reasons does Rory give when he rejects her suggestion?

....

7. Why does Donna ask to see the earrings in the shop?

....

8. What two reasons does Lia give to explain why she feels so upset?

....

9. Why has Donna's dad come to look for her in the park?

....

10. Why does he think Donna couldn't have bought the T-shirts?

....

What happens next?

Read these three suggestions for what happens next.
Explain why they are good ideas or bad ideas. Then choose the way you'd like the play to end.

1

Lia: It's a lie! I would never buy that T-shirt for anyone. Donna stole them. I saw her. I was in the shop when she did it.

I think this is a good idea because

....

....

I think this is a bad idea because

....

....

2

Rory: Actually, Mr Snowdon, it was a present from Donna, not Lia. The shop assistant is a friend of mine and Donna promised to pay her later when she had her purse with her.

Mr Snowdon: Then why did you say it was a present from Lia, Donna?

I think this is a good idea because

....

....

I think this is a bad idea because

....

....

3

Lia: It's not true. I don't know anything about the T-shirt, Mr Snowdon.

Rory: I bought them, Mr Snowdon. It was a present from me. I'm sorry you don't like it. I'll take it back.

I think this is a good idea because

....

....

I think this is a bad idea because

....

....

I think the best ending for the play would be

Language Practice Worksheet 1

1 Discuss which is the best introduction to the story with a partner.

1. We often have to make difficult choices in life. We have to choose between things which are important to us. What is more important to you – truth or friendship?

2. Sometimes our friends do strange things, but loyalty to your friends is the most important thing in life, even when it means telling lies. Do you agree?

3. Is it wrong to listen to private conversations or to spy on your friends? In certain circumstances, this may be OK. What do you think?

2 Imagine these thought bubbles are missing from the play. Match each one to one of the characters in the play.

1 Poor thing. It must be awful to discover your best friend is a thief – and deceiving you at the same time.

....

2 There she is at last! I've been all over town looking for her!

....

3 I wonder why she asked me to show her the earrings – she hardly looked at them when I brought them to her!

....

4 I don't feel like trying anything on now. I just want to get away from here. I feel so shocked.

....

5 That's strange. She told me she bought them – now she's denying it! And she didn't have any money … what's going on?

....

6 I really like him. And I know he likes this T-shirt.

....

Language Practice Worksheet 2

1 In *What happens next?*, Rory makes the following excuse:
The shop assistant is a friend of mine and Donna promised to pay her later when she had her purse with her.
Fill in the missing words in these excuses and then find them in the word search. The remaining letters complete the excuse Rory gave his teacher when he didn't hand in his homework.

> *blown   given*
> *left   dropped   deleted*
> *stolen   spilled   torn*
> *forgotten   fallen*

1. Diana told the physics teacher that she had done the homework project but she didn't have it because she had .... it on the bus.

2. Mark told the English teacher that he had written the essay but he didn't have it because he had .... it in the fire.

3. Henry told the maths teacher that he had done the maths problems but he didn't have them because his baby brother had .... them into twenty pieces.

4. Millie told the music teacher that she had done the homework project but she didn't have it because she had .... to bring it to school with her.

5. Georgina told the history teacher that she had done the essay on the computer but she didn't have it because the computer had .... it.

6. Phil told the geography teacher that he had done the homework project but he didn't have it with him because someone had .... his school bag.

7. Alice told the biology teacher that she had done the experiment but she didn't have the results with her because her exercise book had .... into a puddle and was very wet.

8. Dan told the French teacher that he had done the homework but he didn't have it with him because someone had .... coffee on his book.

9. Maria told the German teacher that she had written the essay in the garden but she didn't have it with her because it had .... away in the wind.

10. Sam told the chemistry teacher that he had done the homework but that he had .... it to the physics teacher by mistake.

← → ↑ ↓ ↘

d	e	l	e	t	e	d	d	f
r	h	e	e	h	a	n	e	o
o	d	f	n'	t	b	e	l	r
p	e	t	a	e	n	v	l	g
p	a	o	b	l	l	i	i	o
e	e	r	t	o	l	g	p	t
d	p	n	r	i	n	e	s	t
t	i	t	b	l	o	w	n	e
o	u	t	s	t	o	l	e	n

Rory told the English teacher that he had written his essay on the computer but

__ __ __ __ __ __ __ __ __ __ __ __ __ __ __

__ __ __ __ __ __ __ __ __ __ __ __ __

2 Now imagine that you are Rory's teacher. What is your answer to him when he gives this excuse?

....

....

9 The Concert

Characters

Write your name next to the character that you play.

Lynne (girl)

_____

Chris (boy, Lynne's boyfriend)

_____

Lynne's mother

_____

Lynne's father

_____

Benedict East (boy)

_____

Suzy (girl, Lynne's friend)

_____

Jake (Chris's older brother)

_____

Scene 1: **At Lynne's house; the last day of the summer holidays.**

Lynne: It's been a fantastic summer hasn't it?

Chris: Yeah. It's a pity we've got to go back to school tomorrow. I've almost forgotten how to write an essay.

Lynne: Don't worry. It'll come back to you quickly! Do you want to know what the best thing about the holidays has been for me?

Chris: What? Tell me.

Lynne: Well, you and I haven't quarrelled at all. I just want to say thank you. It's been a very special summer.

Chris: Yeah, you're right. Let's go out somewhere this evening and enjoy the last moments of our holiday. What's on at the cinema? Have you got the paper?

Lynne: Yes. The cinema information is usually near the back … sport … theatre … music … where are the films? Hey, look at this!

Chris: What is it?

Lynne: "Because of the huge demand for tickets for the Micky Farquin concert at the beginning of September, the organisers have decided to put on one extra concert on the afternoon of Saturday, September 3rd. Tickets are on sale from 1.00 pm on Tuesday 30th August." That's today! What time is it?

Chris: It's almost quarter to one.

Lynne: Brilliant! I'd love to go. I didn't even try when the first tickets went on sale. The whole world was trying to buy tickets. But now there's an extra concert!

Chris: I don't want to see Micky Farquin. I can't stand that kind of music. It's a complete waste of money.

Lynne: Well, I really like him, Chris … Can't you just go, for me?

Chris: No way. I can't think of anything worse.

Lynne: Oh, I just thought … oh well … Look, it's late. I told Dad I'd be back about one. He's cooking Mexican food for lunch…

Chris: OK. I'll walk to the bus stop with you.

Lynne: No, it's alright. It's raining. It's stupid for two of us to get wet. I've got an umbrella.

Chris: But Lynne, what about the cinema … what's wrong?

Lynne: Oh, nothing. I suddenly feel a bit tired, that's all. See you at school tomorrow.

Scene 2: Lynne is having lunch with her parents.

Lynne's dad: How's the food?

Lynne: It's brilliant, Dad. You're a fantastic cook.

Lynne's mum: It's delicious but it's so spicy! Quick, Lynne, can you pour some water for me?

Lynne: Here you are, Mum.

The telephone rings.

Lynne: I'll get it. I've finished eating anyway.

She picks up the phone.

Lynne: 7560-4916. Hello?

Benedict: Can I speak to Lynne, please?

Lynne: Speaking. Who is it?

Benedict: It's Benedict. Benedict East.

Lynne: Oh, hi! What a surprise!

Benedict: Stephanie told me you were a big Micky Farquin fan. It says in the local paper that they are putting on an extra concert. Do you want to come with me? I'm going to try and get tickets today.

Lynne: Oh, I … er … well, thanks for the offer, Benedict, but I should really go with Chris …

Benedict: OK. That's fine. I don't want to come between you and Chris, but if he doesn't want to go … I'll give you a ring later when I've got the tickets. Then you can give me your answer, OK?

Lynne: OK, Benedict. Bye.

She dials Suzy's number.

Suzy: Hello.

Lynne: Suzy? It's me … Lynne.

Suzy: Oh, hi!

Lynne: Guess who just rang me!

Suzy: Brad Pitt?

Lynne: No, don't be stupid … Benedict East!

Suzy: What?! That's even better than Brad Pitt! You must be in heaven! What did he say?

Lynne: He wanted me to go with him to the Micky Farquin concert.

Suzy: You're joking! That's fantastic! I'm so jealous!

Lynne: I'm going to say no.

Suzy: WHAT?!

Lynne: I'm crazy about Micky Farquin, but if I go, I have to go with Chris.

Suzy: And are you going with Chris?

Lynne: Well, no. He says he hates that kind of music. But we've had such a great summer together. I don't want to spoil it all by going out with Benedict. It seems so disloyal to Chris.

Suzy: You're crazy, Lynne. You're going to miss the concert, and you're going to turn down a guy like Benedict! Well, I hope Chris is worth it …

Scene 3: Next day at Chris's brother Jake's flat.

Jake: Hello, you two. Come on in. Have you had a good summer?

Chris: Oh, yeah, it's been great, hasn't it, Lynne?

Lynne: Yes, it has.

Jake: Listen, Chris, I know it's your birthday next week, but I haven't had time to buy you anything, so I want to get you some tickets for a show. What would you like to see? My flatmate works at a ticket agency. He can get me tickets to anything.

Chris: Anything? That's brilliant. I'd love to go to the football match on Saturday afternoon. Can he get tickets for that, for me and Lynne?

Jake: No problem. I'll call him now.

He goes out of the room.

Lynne: You don't care, do you? You know I really want to go to the Micky Farquin concert. You won't come with me, but you expect me to go with you to the football match with you. That's so selfish!

Chris: But it's <u>my</u> birthday present!

Lynne: Well, find someone else to go with you. I'm not coming!

Scene 4: At Lynne's house an hour later.

Lynne's mum: Lynne, is that you? There's a message for you on the answering machine.

Lynne switches on the answering machine.

Benedict: Hi, Lynne. Benedict here. I've managed to get two tickets for the Micky Farquin concert. Call me back if you want to go with me, OK? Bye.

Comprehension check

1. Why has it been a special summer for Lynne?

   ....

2. How does Chris want to spend the end of the holidays?

   ....

3. Why is there going to be an extra Micky Farquin concert?

   ....

4. What is Lynne's reaction to the news about an extra concert?

   ....

5. What does Chris feel about going to the concert?

   ....

6. Lynne makes an excuse and says she's tired. What reason can you give for her sudden change of mood?

   ....

7. Why does Lynne want to say no to Benedict's invitation?

   ....

8. What does Lynne think when Chris asks for tickets to the football game?

   ....

9. What is Chris's reason for his choice of tickets?

   ....

10. Why does Benedict leave a message on Lynne's answering machine?

   ....

What happens next?

Read these three suggestions for what happens next.
Explain why they are good ideas or bad ideas. Then choose the way you'd like the play to end.

1

Scene 5: The next day.

Lynne is on the phone.

Lynne: Chris, it's me. Look, I'm really sorry about our quarrel yesterday. I was being selfish, not you. Of course I'll go with you to the football match. I don't really understand football, but I can always learn about it! And maybe you're right – perhaps Micky Farquin's music isn't that great, after all …

I think this is a good idea because

....
....
....

I think this is a bad idea because

....
....
....
....

2

Lynne picks up the phone and dials Benedict's number

Lynne: Oh hello…is that Benedict? This is Lynne. Yes please! I'd love to go to the concert. I'll meet you at 1.30 at the station.

Scene 5: The next day.

The phone rings.

Lynne: 7560-4916.

Chris: Oh, hi, Lynne. I just wanted to apologise. I've sold the tickets for the football match and guess what … I've bought two tickets for the Micky Farquin concert!

I think this is a good idea because

....
....
....
....

I think this is a bad idea because

....
....
....
....

3

Scene 5: The next day.

Chris is on the phone.

Chris: Is that Darren? Hi, it's Chris here. Listen, Darren, guess what … I've got a spare ticket for the football match on Saturday. Do you want to come? Yes? Great! I'll see you at 1.30 at the station.

I think this is a good idea because

....
....
....
....

I think this is a bad idea because

....
....
....
....

I think the best ending for the play would be

Language Practice Worksheet 1

Read each of these statements about something that happened in the play. If a statement is true, take a letter from the TRUE column. If it is false, take a letter from the FALSE column. Write the letters in the spaces to find the name of the football team that Chris supports.

	TRUE	FALSE
1. Chris and Lynne quarrelled a lot during the holiday.	G	M
2. Chris wants to go to the cinema because it's the last day of the holidays.	A	H
3. The concert is going to be on Tuesday 30th August.	L	N
4. Lynne is crazy about Micky Farquin.	C	P
5. Lynne's dad is making Indian food for lunch.	E	H
6. Chris walks with Lynne to the bus stop.	B	E
7. It's a wet day.	S	Q
8. Lynne's friend is called Katy Marshall.	M	T
9. Suzy thinks Lynne should go to the concert with Benedict.	E	W
10. Chris's older brother lives with him.	Y	R
11. Chris's brother has bought him a wonderful birthday present.	P	U
12. Chris's birthday is in September.	N	O
13. Chris wants four tickets for the football match.	C	I
14. Lynne gets very angry with Jake.	B	T
15. Benedict talks to Lynne on the phone and invites her to the Micky Farquin concert a second time.	S	E
16. Benedict hasn't got tickets for the concert, but he knows a friend who can get them.	N	D

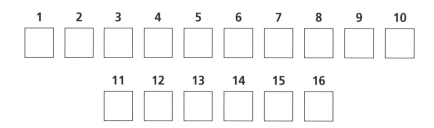

1 2 3 4 5 6 7 8 9 10

11 12 13 14 15 16

Language Practice Worksheet 2

1 Read the following extracts from the play again. Choose a word from
the list which best describes the character's feelings in each extract.

> angry   dismissive   disappointed   complimentary   enthusiastic   diplomatic   sceptical   romantic

1. Lynne: I just want to say thank you. It's been a very special summer.

....

2. Lynne: Brilliant! I'd love to go.

....

3. Chris: No way. I can't think of anything worse.

....

4. Lynne: Oh, nothing. I suddenly feel a bit tired, that's all.

....

5. Lynne: You're a fantastic cook.

....

6. Benedict: I don't want to come between you and Chris.

....

7. Suzy: Well, I hope Chris is worth it …

....

8. Lynne: Well, find someone else to come with you. I'm not coming!

....

2 Benedict is buying tickets for the Micky Farquin concert at the box office.
Put the dialogue in the right order. The first one has been done for you.

☐ How much are the tickets?

☐ OK. I'll take two at £8, please.

☐ Are the £8 seats the cheapest?

[1] Can I help you?

☐ Cash, please.

☐ No, there are tickets at £5, but we've sold out of them.

☐ Yes. We've got a few left.

☐ Right. Here are your tickets. Enjoy the show.

☐ How would you like to pay?

☐ There are some at £15, and some at £8 left.

☐ Yes, have you got any tickets left for the concert?

10 The Favour

Characters

Write your name next to the character that you play.

Emma (girl)

_____

Mike (boy)

_____

Mr Redwood (Emma's father)

_____

Mrs Redwood (Emma's mother)

_____

Mr Griffiths (Mike's father)

_____

Mrs Griffiths (Mike's mother)

_____

Scene 1: On the school bus, Tuesday afternoon.

Emma: Hi, Mike. Can I sit next to you?

Mike: Yeah. I'll just move my school bag. How are things? I haven't seen you for ages.

Emma: I know. I've been so busy.

Mike: What have you been doing?

Emma: I'm in the rowing club, so I have to get up at 6 three days a week for training. We usually have a regatta every Saturday. And I'm in the school play so we're rehearsing two evenings a week after school, and I'm taking my Grade 5 cello exam in a few weeks.

Mike: It sounds like a nightmare!

Emma: Mmm, and there's so much homework to do these days!

Mike: I know. Three history essays before the end of next week ... when are you going to find the time to do those?

Emma: I don't know, Mike. I'm really worried about it, actually. I haven't got time to read all the books and do the research. Have you done them?

Mike: Yes, I've finished two of them, and I've nearly finished the last one.

Emma: Can you do me a favour, Mike?

Mike: Of course. What is it?

Emma: Can I copy some of the stuff from your essays? Mr Maitland won't know. We can say we both used the same books for research.

Mike: Sure. No problem.

Emma: Oh, Mike. You're a star. Remember, I owe you a huge favour now, OK?

Mike: Don't worry! I'm sure I'll need a favour one day. Look, here are the first two essays.

Emma: Thanks. I'll give them back to you tomorrow. Oh, here's my stop! See you tomorrow. Thanks again!

Scene 2: Emma's house, Friday afternoon.

Mr Redwood: Now Emma, are you sure you'll be alright?

Emma: Don't worry, Dad. I've got my three best friends to stay. Josie, Alice and Sal are all very responsible girls. Trust us!

Mrs Redwood: If I were you, I'd forget about the regatta on Saturday, and come and see Grandma instead.

Emma: I can't let the team down, Mum. The regatta is really important. I've got to be there.

Mrs Redwood: *(sighs)* Yes, and it's too far to travel in one day. Anyway, I think you're old enough now to manage on your own for a weekend.

Emma: Of course I am!

Mrs Redwood: And we don't want any more than three friends here ... OK?

Mr Redwood: And definitely no boys.

Emma: Yes, Mum. Yes, Dad.

Mrs Redwood: No more than three friends and no boys, do you promise?

Emma: Yes, of course, I promise.

Mr Redwood: Come on, darling! We must go. We have to buy my mum a present before we set off, remember!

Mrs Redwood: Alright. I'm coming. Take care Emma! We'll phone you when we get there.

Emma and her mum embrace.

Emma: Bye, Mum. Bye, Dad! Safe journey!

Scene 3: As the Redwoods get into their car.

Mrs Redwood: I'm still feeling nervous. Do you think we can trust her?

Mr Redwood: Oh, she'll be fine. She's very sensible.

Mrs Redwood: Well, I don't know ...

Mr Redwood: Now, why don't you forget about it? Just relax and enjoy the drive.

Scene 4: Just after Emma's parents have left, the phone rings. It's Mike.

Mike: Hi, Emma!

Emma: Hi, Mike. Thanks a lot for those essays, by the way. You really helped me out!

Mike: Oh, that's OK. Actually, there's something you could do to help me out ...

Emma: What is it? I owe you a favour!

Mike: Well, there's a great party on tonight at this club just outside the city. I really want to go, but I know my parents won't let me.

Emma: Have you tried asking them?

Mike: No, because I know what they'll say – that I'm not old enough. So, I was thinking ... can I tell them I'm coming over to see you – to keep you company tonight?

Emma: You mean you'll use me as an excuse to go to the party?

Mike: Well, yeah. They'll probably never ask you about it, but just in case they do. Come on, Emma. You owe me a favour.

Emma: Well, OK, then. I just hope they never find out the truth.

Mike: Thanks, Emma!

Scene 5: At a garage, about half an hour later. The Redwoods meet the Griffiths, by chance. Mr Redwood is filling up with petrol.

Mrs Redwood: Hello!

Mrs Griffiths: Oh, hello there! I believe you're on your way to see your mother?

Mr Redwood: Yes, it's her birthday. How did you know?

Mr Griffiths: Oh, Mike told us. That's why he's going round to see Emma tonight. She asked him to go and keep her company. She's on her own, isn't she?

Mrs Redwood: On her own? But ...

Mr Redwood: Are you sure Mike's going to see her tonight?

Mrs Griffiths: Well, that's what he told us. Why? Is there a problem?

Mrs Redwood: It's just that Emma promised us she wouldn't have any boys round tonight. Her three best friends are staying over. I'd be very upset if I found out she had lied to us, that's all.

Mr Griffiths: Why don't you ring her? Here, you can use my mobile.

Mr Redwood: Thanks, Richard.

He takes the mobile and starts dialing.

Mr Redwood: Hello, Emma?

Emma: Dad! Where are you? You can't have got to Grandma's yet!

Mr Redwood: No, we're at the garage. We stopped for some petrol. Guess who we bumped into – Mike's parents! In fact, they're right here with us! They say you've invited Mike round tonight. Is that true?

Emma: *(to herself)* Oh, no. If I tell Dad the truth, Mike will get into serious trouble. And then he might tell them I copied his essays!

Comprehension check

1. What favour does Emma ask Mike?
    ....

2. Why does she need his help?
    ....

3. How will Emma explain to the teacher about the two very similar essays?
    ....

4. Why are Emma's parents going away for the weekend?
    ....

5. Why can't Emma go with them?
    ....

6. What does Emma promise her parents?
    ....

7. How does Emma's father feel about leaving her on her own?
    ....

8. What favour does Mike ask Emma?
    ....

9. Why won't his parents let him go to the party?
    ....

10. Why does Emma's father decide to phone her from the garage?
    ....

What happens next?

Read these three suggestions for what happens next.
Explain why they are good ideas or bad ideas. Then choose the way you'd like the play to end.

1

Emma: No, Dad, of course not. He's just using me as an excuse. He wants to go to a party tonight, but his parents won't let him go. That's why he told them he was coming here. Don't tell them, please. I don't want him to get into trouble.

I think this is a good idea because

....
....
....
....

I think this is a bad idea because

....
....
....
....

2

Emma: No, Dad, of course it's not true. I'll tell you what happened ..

Mr Redwood: Hold on, Mike's father wants to speak to you ...

Mr Griffiths: Emma, I've just thought of something. You don't know anything about a party that Mike wants to go to tonight, do you?

Emma: A party? Um ... I ...

Mr Griffiths: *(to his wife)* I knew it! He's planning to go to that party! Thanks, Keith. *(He hands back the phone to Emma's dad.)* Come on, Julia. We're going home to sort this out with Mike.

I think this is a good idea because

....
....
....
....

I think this is a bad idea because

....
....
....
....

3

Emma: I can explain, Dad. I did invite him over – but it's not what you think. I need some help with my history essays, and he said he'd help me. He isn't going to stay long, I promise.

Mr Redwood: I don't believe your promises any more, Emma! You're obviously not responsible enough to stay at home on your own. You'll have to come with us to Grandma's. We'll be home in half an hour to pick you up.

Emma: But what about the regatta?

Mr Redwood: You should have thought about that before you lied to us.

I think this is a good idea because

....
....
....
....

I think this is a bad idea because

....
....
....
....

I think the best ending for the play would be

Language Practice Worksheet 1

There are several examples in the play, of people giving advice.
Look at these extracts again:

Mrs Redwood: <u>If I were you, I'd</u> forget about the regatta on Saturday.
Mr Redwood: Now, <u>why don't you</u> forget about it? Just relax and enjoy the drive.
Mr Griffiths: <u>Why don't you</u> ring her?
Emma: <u>Have you tried</u> asking them?

Now read these four letters to a problem page. Write four short replies giving advice.

1 **Dear Amanda,**
Last week my sister left her diary on her bed and I read it. I had quite a shock because I learned that she has been taking drugs. I don't know what to do. I know I should tell my parents, but my sister knows I once stole something from my teacher and she'll tell my parents if she finds out I've been reading her diary. What would you do in my situation?
Jake (from London)

Amanda: Dear Jake,
If I were you I would ....
....
....
....

2 **Dear Amanda,**
My best friend thinks about – and talks about – this boy in my school all the time. She adores him and dreams about him at night. He is quite nice to her, and has danced with her once at a school dance. He also sat next to her on the bus on a school trip. The problem is, he phoned me last week and asked me out. We went to the cinema and then had a pizza. He really likes me and I really like him. Should I continue the relationship or give it up out of loyalty to a friend?
Annabel (from Bristol)

Amanda: Dear Annabel,
Perhaps you should ....
....
....
....

3 **Dear Amanda,**
Every day when I walk home from school I see a group of boys who are really rough and aggressive. They shout at me and threaten me, and once they asked me for money and said they had a knife. I didn't see it, but I am really scared and I don't want to go out of the house. I am sure they are planning to do something awful to me. I feel stupid because I am sixteen years old and I don't want to tell my parents or my friends because they will think I am being silly. It has ruined my social life and I make excuses when friends invite me out. I can't ask my parents to walk to the bus stop with me each time I go out! What can I do?
Mark (from Cardiff)

Amanda: Dear Mark,
Have you tried ....
....
....
....

4 **Dear Amanda,**
I've just moved to a new school and I don't have any friends. Everyone seems to be in a little group of friends, and all these groups do things together at lunchtime and during the break. Are they unfriendly - or perhaps it's me? What am I doing wrong?
Jason (from Brighton)

Amanda: Dear Jason,
Why don't you ....
....
....
....

Language Practice Worksheet 2

1 Read the following sentences from the play again.
Match each one to one of the functions in the list below.
Write the function next to the sentence.

persuading advising promising commiserating explaining reassuring hesitating agreeing

1. **Mike:** It sounds like a nightmare! ....

2. **Mike:** Sure. No problem. ....

3. **Emma:** I'll give them back to you tomorrow. ....

4. **Mrs Redwood:** If I were you, I'd forget about the regatta ... .

5. **Emma:** I can't let the team down, Mum. ....

6. **Mr Redwood:** Oh, she'll be fine. ....

7. **Mrs Redwood:** Well, I don't know. ....

8. **Mike:** Come on, Emma. ....

2 Now write a response to each sentence using the function given in brackets.
You might find some of the words or phrases in the sentences above useful.

1. You mustn't be late tomorrow.

   (promising) ....

2. Can you do me a favour?

   (agreeing) ....

3. My boyfriend doesn't pay me enough attention.

   (advising) ....

4. I really think you should come to the party.

   (explaining) ....

5. My parents are always criticising me, and my brother is always fighting with me.

   (commiserating) ....

6. I don't feel like going out tonight. I'm really depressed about my schoolwork.

   (persuading) ....

7. Could you lend me your camera for the weekend? I know it's expensive, but I'll look after it.

   (hesitating) ....

8. I'm really worried about Jenny. She's not eating well, and she's getting very thin.

   (reassuring) ....

11 Ten-Pin Bowling

Characters

Write your name next to the character that you play.

Jason (boy)

_____

Catherine (girl, Jason's friend and neighbour)

_____

Mrs Scott (Jason's mother)

_____

Mr Scott (Jason's father)

_____

Mr McCarthy (Catherine's father)

_____

Sonia (girl)

_____

Russell (boy, Sonia's boyfriend)

_____

Scene 1: At Jason's house.

Jason: Mum! You haven't forgotten about tonight, have you?

Mrs Scott: Remind me ... you're going out ...

Jason: Yes, I'm going bowling.

Mr Scott: Oh Jason, do you have to? You know the bowling alley isn't in a nice part of town, and it's a long way away.

Jason: I know the area's a bit rough, but the bowling alley is great. The people who go there are fine. They're friendly and I feel completely safe.

Mrs Scott: Yes, but we worry about your journey home. I don't want you to wait around for buses. I'm going to give you money for a taxi home.

Mr Scott: We want you home before eleven o'clock tonight, do you understand? You've got exams soon.

Jason: Alright, Dad, I promise I'll be home before 11.

Mrs Scott: How are you going to get there? By bus?

Jason: No, Catherine's dad's taking us there by car.

The doorbell rings.

Jason: They're here. See you later!

They drive away.

Catherine: Wish me luck tonight, Jason. I'm feeling really nervous.

Jason: Why's that?

Catherine: I'm playing against Sonia. It's only a friendly game organised by the youth club but Sonia and I have always been enemies – and not only in bowling, either ...

Catherine's dad: You'll do fine! But remember, home before 11, OK? Here, I'll give you some money for a taxi.

Jason: It's OK, Mr McCarthy, I've got money for a taxi. Catherine can share one with me. And I've got to be home before 11, too!

Catherine's dad: That's good! Thanks, Jason. Take care!

Jason and Catherine: Bye!

Scene 2: At the bowling alley.

Catherine: Oh look! Sonia's here already. She's over there with her boyfriend, Russell.

Jason: Is he her boyfriend? He's such a creep! Oh, no, he's coming over to speak to us.

Russell: So you've decided to come, have you?

Catherine: What do you mean?

Russell: Well, you know you're going to lose, don't you?

Jason: She's not going to lose! Catherine's the best!

Russell: Do you want a bet? Or are you too scared you might be wrong?

Jason: I'm not scared! I know I'm right. OK, I'll make a bet with you.

Jason takes his taxi money out of his wallet and puts it on the table.

There! I bet you £10 Catherine's going to win.

Russell: You seem very sure of yourself! Here's my £10. Winner takes all!

Russell puts his money on the table too, and puts a bag on top of it.

Catherine: Jason! That's the money for the taxi! What will happen if I lose? How will we get home?

Jason: Well, you'd better not lose!

Catherine: OK. Let's start.

An hour and a half later.

Catherine: Well, we're equal – one game each.

Sonia: I need a break before the final game.

Russell: Yeah, let's go and get some coffee.

As Catherine and Jason walk off, Sonia and Russell disappear, taking the money. Catherine and Jason don't notice. 15 minutes later.

Catherine: Jason, have you seen Russell and Sonia? They were just going to get a coffee. They've been gone for ages!

Jason: I'll go and look for them.

15 minutes later.

Catherine: Jason, where have you been? Look at the time! It's nearly 11 o'clock!

Jason: I can't find them anywhere; they must have gone outside for some fresh air.

Catherine: Oh no! We can't wait for them any longer. And they've taken the money! How are we going to get home?

Jason: Have you got any money at all?

Catherine: Well, just some small change. How about you?

Jason: I might have enough for the bus fare.

Catherine: My parents don't want me to catch a bus from here.

Jason: No, mine don't either. And we'll never make it home by 11 if we don't get a taxi ...

Comprehension check

1. Where is Jason planning to go?

   ....

2. What kind of an area is the bowling alley in?

   ....

3. How is Jason going to get home?

   ....

4. How is Jason going to get to the bowling alley?

   ....

5. What time must Jason be home by?

   ....

6. Why doesn't Mr Scott want Jason to be late?

   ....

7. Why is Catherine feeling nervous?

   ....

8. What kind of relationship do Sonia and Catherine have?

   ....

9. What does Jason do to prove how confident he is in Catherine?

   ....

10. Why can't Catherine and Jason get their money back from the bet?

   ....

What happens next?

Read these three suggestions for what happens next.
Explain why they are good ideas or bad ideas. Then choose the way you'd like the play to end.

1

Catherine:	We'll have to phone our parents, Jason.
Jason:	They'll be furious if they know I bet the money!
Catherine:	We can tell them Sonia and Russell stole it from inside your bag.

I think this is a good idea because

....

....

I think this is a bad idea because

....

....

2

Catherine:	Well, we'll have to get a bus. We'll be late, but we can always say we had to wait a long time for a taxi ...
Jason:	Yes, at least they won't find out about the bet.

I think this is a good idea because

....

....

I think this is a bad idea because

....

....

3

Catherine:	Let's get a taxi anyway, and when we get home, we'll pretend to discover that your wallet's been stolen. I'm sure my Dad will have some more money to pay the taxi driver.

I think this is a good idea because

....

....

I think this is a bad idea because

....

....

I think the best ending for the play would be (   )

Language Practice Worksheet 1

Jason and Catherine are trying to arrange to go bowling again. Here is Catherine's diary for the next few days. Jason is suggesting some possible times. They need an hour and a half to play a game. Write in Catherine's replies using *going to*.

Basketball practice lasts for an hour and a half. She goes running for 45 minutes. The journey to her grandmother's house takes 30 minutes. Her guitar lesson is half an hour long, and the theatre performance lasts two hours.

	Monday	Tuesday	Wednesday	Thursday	Friday	Saturday	Sunday
18.00	basketball practice	meet Joe for a quick coffee	go running	early supper	early supper	go running	visit Grandma
19.00			guitar lesson	theatre	meet Tim		
20.00	supper		supper				Anna's party
21.00	bed (early night)	cinema	write essay		Cascades nightclub	dinner (Jason)	

1. How about nine o'clock on Monday?
   No, because I'm going to have an early night.
   ....

2. How about eight o'clock on Thursday?
   ....
   ....

3. How about seven thirty on Friday?
   ....
   ....

4. How about eight o'clock on Tuesday?
   ....
   ....

5. How about eight thirty on Sunday?
   ....
   ....

6. How about seven fifteen on Wednesday?
   ....
   ....

7. How about six thirty on Saturday?
   ....
   ....

8. How about seven o'clock on Monday?
   ....
   ....

9. How about eight thirty on Thursday?
   ....
   ....

10. How about nine o'clock on Tuesday?
    ....
    ....

11. How about nine o'clock on Wednesday?
    ....
    ....

12. How about six thirty on Sunday?
    ....
    ....

When can Catherine and Jason play their game?

They can play at .... or at ....

Language Practice Worksheet 2

1 Read these sentences from the play again.
Choose the best definition for each of the underlined words or expressions.

1. The area's a bit **rough**.
   (a) The area isn't smooth.
   (b) The area is a bit dangerous.

2. He's a **creep**.
   (a) He crawls along the ground.
   (b) He is an unpleasant person.

3. You're very **sure of yourself**!
   (a) You are confident.
   (b) You are sure you are yourself.

4. **Winner takes all!**
   (a) The winner gets all the money.
   (b) The winner wins all the games.

5. I've got some **small change**.
   (a) I've changed in some small ways.
   (b) I've got some coins.

2 Follow the directions on the map and mark the location of the bowling alley.

From Jason's house, turn left, and at the crossroads, left again. Go over the bridge, and take the second right, just before the traffic lights.　Go under the railway bridge and, just after the second entrance to the park, turn sharp left. Go straight along to the end of this road, and follow the bend to the right. Go round the roundabout, taking the second exit, and the bowling alley is on the corner, on your left.

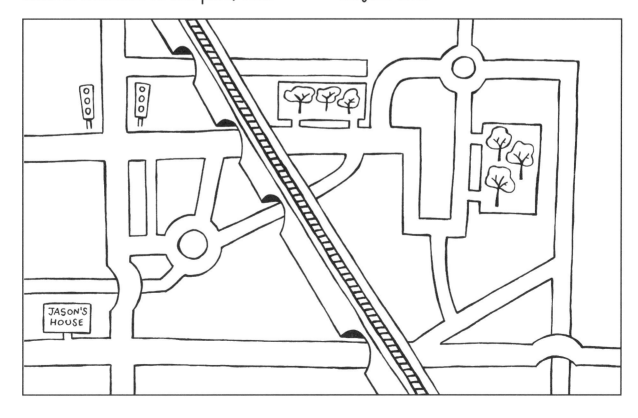

12 The Boy Next Door

Characters

Write your name next to the character that you play.

Michelle (girl) _____

Dan (boy) _____

Geoff (boy) _____

Scene 1: **In the garden of Michelle's house. Michelle and Dan are talking over the fence.**

Michelle: Hi. Do you live there?

Dan: Yes. Are you our new neighbour?

Michelle: Yes. I'm Michelle. What's your name?

Dan: It's Dan.

Michelle: We've just moved in. We've come from Grimsby. My dad's just changed jobs. I don't know anyone here. Have you lived here long?

Dan: I was born here ... not in this house, but about a mile away.

Michelle: Do you want to come over for coffee?

Dan: OK. I'll just climb over the fence.

He jumps over.

Michelle: What's it like round here?

Dan: Oh, not bad.

Michelle: I'm starting at the new school next week. Which school do you go to?

Dan: I go to Larkswell School.

Michelle: Oh, great! That's where I'm going. I don't even know what it looks like.

Dan: I'll show you if you like. We can walk over there tomorrow ... if you're free, that is. I can show you the town as well.

Michelle: Oh, Dan, that would be great! Thanks a lot.

Scene 2: The next day, in the town centre.

Dan: This is a great bookshop. And the music shop is over there, next to that big office block.

Michelle: We've walked miles! Shall we have a drink? Where's a good place?

Dan: There's a really nice new café just round the corner.

Michelle: Right! Lead me to it!

Michelle and Dan are in the café.

Michelle: I love all these magazines everywhere! Do you like reading, Dan?

Dan: I love it! I'm always reading.

Michelle: What's your favourite book?

Dan: I enjoyed *The Beach* a lot.

Michelle: Me, too. What's your favourite film?

Dan: I loved *Sixth Sense*.

Michelle: I don't believe it! That's my favourite film, too!

Dan: What a coincidence!

Michelle: How far is the school from here?

Dan: About five minutes.

Michelle: Come on, I want to have a look at it.

They leave and walk down the road.

Dan: Well, here we are! Larkswell. I think you'll like it.

Michelle: How big is it?

Dan: There are about 1,000 students.

Michelle: And these are the playing fields ... do you play any sports, Dan?

Dan: No, I'm hopeless at sports. I'm in the computer club, though, and the technology club. At the moment we're designing a robot.

Michelle: You must be very clever!

Dan: Oh, no, I'm just interested in things like that.

Michelle: What's the social life like at this school?

Dan: Social life? What do you mean?

Michelle: Well, are there lots of parties? Do people go out in groups, to clubs and stuff like that?

Dan: I guess so ... I don't get invited to things, but I think there are exciting things going on. I'm sure you'll have a great social life.

Scene 3: The last day of the holidays, Dan knocks on Michelle's door.

Michelle: Hi Dan.

Dan: Hi!

Michelle: Are you busy?

Dan: No, why?

Michelle: Do you want to come for a walk?

Dan: Yes, OK.

Michelle: So ... my first day at my new school tomorrow!

Dan: Yes ...

Michelle: What's up? You look very serious all of a sudden.

Dan: Well ... I ... er ... I was wondering ... Would you like to come out with me on Saturday night? I'd like you to meet some of my friends. I usually go to a chess club on Saturday evenings. Why don't you come with me?

Michelle: Thank you, Dan ... I'd ... I'd ... well, yes, I'd love to go with you.

Scene 4: Outside the school gate on the first day of term.

Michelle: Dan! Dan! I'm over here!

Dan: How was it?

Michelle: Fantastic! Let's walk home together.

Dan: Have you made any new friends?

Michelle: Oh yes! You were right. Everyone is so friendly. Oh, isn't that Geoff from my class over there? The one who looks like a film star?

Dan: Yes. He's the captain of the school gymnastics team.

Geoff: Michelle!

Michelle: Hi.

Geoff: I'm having a party this Saturday evening ... and, well, I really want you to come. I want you to meet everyone. Can you come?

Dan coughs nervously.

Dan: Oh, um ... I ...

Geoff: Not you, nerdy! There aren't going to be any robots there! Hey, come on, Michelle. Do you want me to come and pick you up?

Comprehension check

1. Where is Michelle at the start of the play?

   ....

2. Where does Dan take Michelle the next day?

   ....

3. What kind of things have Dan and Michelle got in common?

   ....

4. Why doesn't Dan play sports?

   ....

5. What are Dan's interests?

   ....

6. Why doesn't he know what kind of social life there is at the school?

   ....

7. What does Dan invite Michelle to on Saturday night?

   ....

8. How does Michelle feel about her first day at school?

   ....

9. What does Geoff invite Michelle to on Saturday night?

   ....

10. Why doesn't Geoff invite Dan too?

    ....

What happens next?

Read these three suggestions for what happens next.
Explain why they are good ideas or bad ideas. Then choose the way you'd like the play to end.

1

Michelle: I'd ... I'd love to come to the party, Geoff. Can you pick me up? I live at 32 Park Avenue.

Geoff: Great. See you on Saturday, then, at about eight.

Geoff leaves.

Michelle: Oh, Dan, I'm so sorry ... I hope you understand. It's a good chance for me to make friends with everyone in my class. We live next door to one another, so I can see you any day I want!

I think this is a good idea because
....
....
....
....

I think this is a bad idea because
....
....
....
....

2

Michelle: Well, I sort of promised ... how about if I go *after* the chess club, Dan?

Geoff: Chess club? You're going to the chess club with Dan? Sorry, I must have made a mistake. I thought you'd be the kind of girl who liked parties and having fun.

Michelle: Oh, I love parties!

Geoff: Well, what are you doing with *him*, then? He's a weirdo!

I think this is a good idea because
....
....
....
....

I think this is a bad idea because
....
....
....
....

3

Michelle: I'd love to come, Geoff. But Dan already asked me to go to the chess club with him. Is it OK if I bring him with me to the party, after his chess game is over?

Geoff: Well ... sure, if you really want to bring Dan ... See you there, then.

Geoff leaves.

Dan: Wow! Thanks, Michelle. I've never been invited to any parties before.

I think this is a good idea because
....
....
....

I think this is a bad idea because
....
....
....

I think the best ending for the play would be

Language Practice Worksheet 1

1   **Look at the play again and find the answers.**

1. Find someone in this play who has lived in a different town.

   Answer: ....

2. Find someone in this play who is good at gymnastics.

   Answer: ....

3. Find someone whose dad has changed jobs.

   Answer: ....

4. Find someone who has always lived in the same town.

   Answer: ....

5. Find someone who has read the book *The Beach*.

   Answer: ....

6. Find someone who has just started a new school.

   Answer: ....

7. Find someone who has just moved house.

   Answer: ....

8. Find someone who has never been invited to any parties at school.

   Answer: ....

2   **Now go round your class. Ask: *Have you ever? ...***

	Name
1. Find someone who has ridden a camel.	
2. Find someone who has eaten raw fish.	
3. Find someone who has been to America.	
4. Find someone who has acted in a play.	
5. Find someone who has read an English novel (in English).	
6. Find someone who has written a letter to a magazine or newspaper.	
7. Find someone who has skied down a black piste.	
8. Find someone who has eaten English food.	
9. Find someone who has spent more than a week in hospital.	
10. Find someone who has been to California.	
11. Find someone who has spoken to a famous film star.	
12. Find someone who has drunk champagne.	

Language Practice Worksheet 2

Put these events from the play in the correct order.
Then match each event to one of the thought bubbles a – h.

☐ Michelle is invited by Geoff to a party.

☐ Dan tells Michelle he doesn't get invited to things.

☐ Michelle's dad tells her they are moving.

☐ Michelle is invited by Dan to the chess club.

☐ Dan meets Michelle.

☐ Michelle listens to Dan talking about the robot he's designing at the technology club.

☐ Michelle and Dan discuss films and books.

☐ Dan offers to show Michelle around town.

b I wonder if she's the new neighbour ...

a Now she'll probably think I'm boring.

c What a great way to meet people – and I really fancy him ...

e Chess is really dull, but he's so nice. I should go.

d We both like the same things!

f She's really nice, so easy to talk to.

g I hope she'll make new friends easily.

h He must be really brainy.

Using Timesaver Plays

Using drama in the EFL classroom

With drama, students are invited to get inside the characters and actually become them. By unlocking their feelings and feeding their imaginations, drama gives students a natural way to learn English. The language helps create a scene or a story; it is not just being studied for its own sake.

All of these short plays are based on situations that young people can relate to. We hope that this will enable students to empathise with the characters and explore their own feelings about the problem situations in the plays.

Knowing the physical restrictions of many classrooms and the time constrictions of most courses, these short plays can be treated as dramatised playreadings as well as recorded on tape or video or performed on a public stage.

The open-ended nature of each play gives you an excellent opportunity for extension work, both discussion and writing.

Warm-up games

In order to perform plays that deal with sensitive issues, your students will need to feel comfortable both with you and with one another. We therefore suggest that before you start a play you use some of the warm-up games that follow with your students.

Number relay

Seat everyone in a large circle and give each student a number (you yourself are number one). In a slow rhythm, get everyone to clap their hands once on their thighs, then clap their hands, then, on the third beat, as they click their fingers, you say your number, "one" and on the fourth beat, while they click their fingers again, you say the number of someone else in the group. Without missing a beat, everyone then claps their thighs, claps their hands, and the new student says his/her own number on the third beat (while everyone clicks their fingers

once), and the student calls out a new number while everyone clicks their fingers a second time. The rhythm mustn't be broken. If a student breaks the rhythm, he/she becomes number one. This way, people have to remember which number is missing.

Chinese whispers

Sit in a circle and whisper a sentence to the person sitting on your left. S/he then whispers it to the next student, and so on, until it comes back to the student on your right who then has to tell the group what they think they have just heard. Sample sentences could be:
Last night I had a terrible dream about a great big yellow monster.
Tomorrow I'm going to have an operation on my nose.
She stood at the door of Mrs Smith's fish sauce shop.
A rat ran by the river with a piece of raw liver.
I really love my Swiss wristwatch.
I'd like a box of mixed biscuits please.
(The last four are tongue-twisters.)

What have they got?

Students separate into pairs. They each have to enact a situation (Student A doesn't speak but it is understood that they have just said something and have to look as if they believe what they have just said.) Student B says: "Thank you" in a way which fits how they would feel in that situation. They can of course move about a bit if the situation calls for it but Student B must say no more than "Thank you". Each pair is given their situation on two slips of paper before they perform. The rest of the class speculates on what the situation is and tries to guess in the shortest possible time. (This can be done as a team game.)

The situations are as follows:
Situation 1
Student A: You have just told Student B that they have got the most wonderful hair that you have ever seen in your life.
Student B: You have just been told that you have got the most wonderful hair in the world.

Situation 2
Student A: You are a postman and you give a letter to Student B.
Student B: The postman gives you a letter which is a bill for a lot more money than you have got in your bank account.

Situation 3
Student A: You give a present to Student B.
Student B: You receive a present...but it is something which you gave to a friend of Student A a long time ago.

Situation 4
Student A: You are a film director. You have just told Student B that they have got the leading part in a Hollywood film.
Student B: You have just been given the leading part in a Hollywood film.

Situation 5
Student A: You have just told Student B s/he is on the wrong train.
Student B: Student A has just told you that you are on the wrong train.

Situation 6
Student A: You are an elderly person. You have just stood up and given your seat on the bus to Student B who doesn't look well.
Student B: You don't feel well; an older person has just stood up to give you their seat on the bus.

Situation 7
Student A: You have just presented an envelope to Student B. It says they have won a prize in a competition – but it is a silly prize: a tin of baked beans.
Student B: You have just received an envelope telling you you have won a prize in a competition; but it's a booby prize – a tin of baked beans.

Preparation

Before you give out any scripts, introduce the topic by way of a discussion with a few questions.

Here are possible opening questions to get your students into the right frame of mind. Only do these publicly if your students are confident with you and with one another about revealing personal things. Otherwise, get your students working in pairs or students can simply be asked to read, understand and think about their answers to the questions for themselves.

1 The Exam
1. Have you ever gone into an exam confident that you know everything?
2. Have you ever gone into an exam having done no revision?
3. Have you ever dreamed that you were taking an exam?
4. Have you ever cheated in a test?
5. Have you ever seen (or been told about) a friend cheating in a test?
6. Is it better to revise for exams alone or with a friend?

2 The Fur Coat
1. Are you the member of a charity?
2. Have you ever raised money for charity? How?
3. Have you ever made a speech?
4. Have you (or has anyone in your family) got any clothes made from real fur?
5. Have you ever been embarrassed by a member of your family?

3 Oliver's Diary
1. Have you ever kept a diary?
2. How long did you manage to keep writing it?
3. How would you feel if you knew someone had read it?
4. Have you ever gone through someone's private things (in a bag/drawer/desk)?
5. Have you ever kept important information or facts from someone?

4 Summer Camp
1. How old were you the first time you went away without your parents?
2. Have you ever been to summer camp? What was good/bad about it?

3. Have you ever risked getting into trouble for someone that you like a lot?
4. Have you ever witnessed an accident?
5. Have you ever had your photo in the newspapers?

5 The Secret
1. Have you ever spent time with someone who is a little bit deaf? How did it make you feel?
2. Have you ever been to a nightclub? What was it like?
3. Have you ever been anywhere where it has been difficult to hear or difficult to understand what was being said to you?
4. Have you ever lied to a friend to avoid doing something you didn't want to do?
5. Have you ever worshipped someone from afar and then found that they also liked you a lot?

6 The Charity Box
1. Have you ever been to a Christmas party? If so, was it enjoyable?
2. Have you ever had a job?
3. Do you ever buy designer clothes? Why / why not?
4. Have you ever tried to collect money for charity?
5. Have you ever given a lot of money to charity?
6. Have you ever spent a large amount of money on a boyfriend/girlfriend?

7 The Joke
1. Do you believe in ghosts?
2. Have you ever met anyone who has seen a ghost?
3. Would you mind spending a night alone in an old house in the countryside?
4. Are you superstitious?
5. Have you ever played a practical joke on anyone?
6. Have you ever been the victim of a practical joke? How did you feel?

8 Friendship and Lies
1. Do you ever feel that schoolwork is spoiling your social life?
2. Have you ever been pressurized or bullied into doing something by a friend?
3. Have you ever stolen anything from a shop?

4. Has a friend of yours ever stolen anything?
5. Have you ever worn a T-shirt with a rude slogan on it?
6. What's the cleverest/funniest thing you have ever seen on a T-shirt?

9 The Concert
1. What's the best concert you've ever been to?
2. Have you ever gone to a sports event/opera/play/concert, etc, just to impress a boyfriend/girlfriend?
3. Have you ever accepted an invitation, then been offered something better and cancelled the first one?
4. What's the best birthday present you have ever had?
5. What's your ideal birthday present?

10 The Favour
1. Have you ever got involved in too many things apart from school work (clubs, sports, extra classes, etc)?
2. Have you ever invited lots of friends back to your house while your parents were out?
3. Have you ever asked a friend for a big favour? Have you ever done a friend a big favour?
4. Have your parents ever left you alone in your house for one or more nights?
5. What is the perfect way to spend a night when you are alone in the house?

11 Ten-Pin Bowling
1. Is there a part of your town which your parents consider dangerous?
2. Have you ever been there, despite their anxiety?
3. Are your parents strict about the time that you have to return home?
4. Have you ever arrived home much later than you promised? What happened?

12 The Boy Next Door
1. Have you always lived in the same house?
2. Where does your family come from?
3. Have you ever changed schools?

4. Have you ever made friends with someone who has joined your class as a new pupil?
5. What is the worst thing about changing schools?
6. Has a friend ever ignored you or betrayed you? What was your reaction? How was the problem resolved?

Language work

Once you have read the play, give out the *What Happens Next?* worksheets and let people fill them in. Collect them in and have two students count the results.

Let your students do the *Comprehension check* and the *Language Practice Worksheets* either in class or for homework.

In addition, they may like to have general discussions about the different value judgements they have given to each optional ending. If you want them to do some extra writing practice, they can do some guided writing, providing some additional endings. They can either do this individually as a written exercise, or in groups, using improvisation techniques. The latter depends on them having very good and fluent language skills.

The performance

It is totally up to you and the class whether or not you want to do the play moving around as if on stage, or simply give a dramatised reading. You may want to get some groups performing the play in front of the rest of the class or you may like to record each group's performance on a cassette recorder or a video tape. Whatever the situation, it will probably help if someone acts as an announcer, introducing each scene and saying what the time lapse is, e.g. *"Scene 4: The examination hall 1¹/₂ hours later"*. If you are doing the play as a dramatized reading, it is good to aim at Michael West's read-and-look-up method. Students should look at their lines briefly, and then look up when they say them. Apart from it being more interesting for the people who are not acting, it also helps the actors learn their lines very quickly.

Stage performance

It is only advisable to give a stage performance of the play if the students are prepared to learn the lines by heart. If everyone is enthusiastic about this, you can spend quite a bit of discussion time deciding how best to stage the play, e.g. *How can we create the forest? Do we just use three or four desks for the scene in the examination hall? How do you suggest we do the scene where Nick makes his speech to the whole school? How can we create the shop where Donna steals the T-shirt?*

You can use this as another opportunity for group work. Split the class into groups and get them to decide how best a particular scene will be staged; what props are needed; what the actors' movements should be; how the lines should be delivered; what their facial expressions should be; how the characters are feeling during the scene being studied, etc. They can discuss their various interpretations until they reach a consensus of agreement. At this point, there will be quite a lot of discussion about the personalities and motives of the characters because this affects how the lines are said. Since your students will already have had to think a lot about motivation in order to decide on a suitable ending for each play, they will already be quite well-prepared for this. If there are two very different opinions about how some lines should be said, the group should try it out with two (or more) groups of actors, to see which version works best.

Various people within the group can take turns at improvising the scene, the essential thing to remember being that they do not have to reproduce the exact words, simply the main sentiment behind the dialogue.

If the play is being recorded, the group needs to brainstorm ideas about musical accompaniment, sound effects, etc, and someone in the group needs to take technical responsibility for how it is all going to be done. There are quite a lot of examples of characters thinking aloud in these playlets. How is that going to be done? Is another voice (off-stage)

going to say the lines while the performing character simply stares quietly and thoughtfully ahead? Is there some way of putting an 'echo' over the voice to indicate that it is not normal speech if you are recording the play on a cassette recorder?

Making a film

Whereas a stage performance will mean the actors learning quite long speeches in a foreign language, performing for the video camera is a much better solution. The film is then shot in short bursts, so that the memorising of text does not become too much of a problem. It also means that students can spend quite a long time setting the scene each time it changes. They may even be prepared to go out on location to film certain sequences, e.g. to the park or to a shop. If you have a particularly gifted group, and several camcorders available to you, you could get different groups to film more than one of the plays and have a mini film festival. This would be a full-scale project and would need several weeks of intense work.

If you have already got to the point where your pupils want to perform the play, then there will be no shortage of ideas on staging. All you need is time – lots of it, but it will be worth the effort – all the students who take part will have indelible memories of this English project work, and any student who has had to learn a role by heart will find that the language that they learned for the role will stick with them in a way that nothing else does.

Answers

1 The Exam
Page 4: Comprehension check
1. Kelly promised that she would revise for the chemistry exam with Maria.
2. Because she is going out with Tom.
3. By reminding her that they still have three weeks left for revision before the exam.
4. Because he dropped chemistry last year.
5. Because he is having a bad effect on Kelly's schoolwork.
6. He asks her if there is a problem.
7. She feels terrible.
8. He thinks he can answer them.
9. The teacher tells them that they will fail the exam if they are caught cheating.
10. She thinks that Tom is cheating.

Page 6: Language Practice Worksheet 1
Exercise 1:
1. cheerful 2. apologetic
3. unenthusiastic 4. reasonable
5. accusing 6. reassuring.
Exercise 2:
1 – c; 2 – b; 3 – c; 4 – c; 5 – a; 6 – b.

Page 7: Language Practice Worksheet 2
Exercise 1:
1 – angry; 2 – thirsty; 3 – hungry;
4 – tired; 5 – cheerful; 6 – miserable;
7 – beautiful; 8 – frightening;
9 – nervous; 10 – frightened.
The theme of the play is: *friendship*.
Exercise 2:
Picture C does not illustrate any of the themes of the play because it shows a family. Picture A shows a group of friends and picture B shows a boyfriend and girlfriend.

2 The Fur Coat
Page 10: Comprehension check
1. A charity concert.
2. *Animals First.*
3. Lots of people care about animals and young people can relate to a charity like that.
4. Because he hasn't started writing his speech yet.
5. They give him ideas and he types them into his computer.
6. That meat is murder.
7. That fur coats are a crime against nature.
8. Becuase she's a bit deaf.
9. She thinks it's disgusting.
10. They laugh and whisper.

Page 12: Language Practice Worksheet 1
1. thyme, 2. piece, 3. sore, 4. seen,
5. caught, 6. bear, 7. hire, 8. fort,
9. write, 10. bored.
The word is **vegetarian**.

Page 13: Language Practice Worksheet 2
Exercise 1:
1(c) 2(c) 3(a) 4(c) 5(a)
Exercise 2:
a) organisation; b) proudly
c) suggestion; d) natural;
e) charitable; f) musician.

3 Oliver's Diary
Page 16: Comprehension check
1. Jenny is talking about how good Lily is at schoolwork and Lily feels embarrassed and wants to change the subject.
2. No, he doesn't. She adores him from a distance.
3. She thinks he might have some photos of himself.
4. So that she can warn Jenny if someone is coming.
5. Two tickets for the Bobby Fillingham concert.
6. Because Mr Park walked into the classroom.
7. Mr Park takes it away.
8. He doesn't want Mr Park to read his diary because it's private.
9. Because the tickets for the Bobby Fillingham concert aren't in the diary.
10. He thinks that Mr Park has stolen the tickets.

Page 18: Language Practice Worksheet 1
Exercise 1:
4, 7, 3, 8, 1, 9, 5, 6, 2.

Page 19: Language Practice Worksheet 2
Exercise 1:
1-11, 2-14, 3-15, 4-9, 5-13, 6-16, 7-10, 2-7, 9-17, 1-12.
The pop group is **Five**.
Exercise 2:
1. happened 2. went 3. opened 4. had
5. didn't have 6. saw 7. had to give
8. gave 9. weren't 10. had disappeared
11. felt 12. discovered 13. had looked
14. am going 15. is.

4 Summer Camp
Page 22: Comprehension check
1. Mr Redwood thinks that Andy is a bad influence on Gemma and that since she met him her behaviour has changed for the worse.

2. They think that Andy and Gemma are too young to be serious about each other.
3. 60 miles away.
4. Andy is going to ride his dad's old motobike to the camp where Gemma is staying.
5. Andy is going to ring Gemma on her mobile when he arrives in Elsam forest.
6. Because the car might catch fire.
7. They use their clothes to keep them warm and comfortable and use a first aid kit on their injuries.
8. Gemma and Andy standing in front of the motorbike.
9. Because she doesn't want her parents to find out that she has been spending time with Andy.
10. Because he doesn't want his father to find out that he has taken his motorbike.

Page 24: Language Practice Worksheet 1
1. I'll meet you. (F) 2. I'll get you out. (I)
3. Nobody will ever know. (R) 4. I'll bring a picnic. (E) 5. I'll already be home and they won't guess what I've been doing. (W) 6. the ambulance will soon be here. (O) 7. I'll have my mobile with me. (R) 8. I think it'll catch fire. (K) 9. you'll catch a cold. (P) 10. he'll take you to the police station and ask you some serious questions. (A) 11. I'll probably be late. (R) 12. he'll go mad. (T) 13. and everyone will return home. (Y).
The letters spell the words: **firework party**.

Page 25: Language Practice Worksheet 2
a) windsurfing b) canoeing
c) trampolining d) cycling e) abseiling
f) writing g) volleyball h) painting
i) pottery j) drama

5 The Secret
Page 28: Comprehension check
1. Because the new DJ who made an album in Ibiza is going to be there.
2. Because she has been hearing strange noises in her ears and she can't always hear what people are saying.
3. For three or four months.
4. That she avoids situations where there is loud music or noise.
5. Because it would ruin their friendship.
6. Because he's the lead singer in a band.
7. He invites Sarah to his band's gig on Saturday.

8. Because she can't go to a noisy concert and she doesn't want to explain why to Joel.
9. It is implied that Eddie is in love with Sarah.
10. Because Eddie is a good friend of Sarah's.

Page 30: Language Practice Worksheet 1
I'm really thirsty. – Let's go for a nice cool drink.
I've got nothing to wear. – Why don't we go on a big shopping trip?
I need some exercise. – How about going swimming?
I've got a bad back. – What about going to the doctor?
I want to go on holiday somewhere hot. – Why don't you go to Greece?
My feet are hurting. – Why don't you soak your feet in hot water?
I haven't got any money. – Let's do the lottery.
I can't speak Spanish. – How about going to Spanish evening classes?
I don't like rap music. – What about turning the radio off?
I'm lonely in this house. – Why don't you get a cat or a dog for company?
I've got hayfever. – Let's take all the flowers out of the room.
I'm really tired. – What about having a little sleep?
It's my birthday next week. – Let's have a party.
The flat is very untidy. – Why don't we tidy it?
Joel's band is called **Static friction**.

Page 31: Language Practice Worksheet 2
Exercise 1
1 (b) **2** (a) **3** (a) **4** (a) **5** (c)
Exercise 2
awful – wonderful
crowded – empty
permanent – temporary
strange – familiar
thorough – quick
upset – calm
worried – carefree

6 The Charity Box
Page 34: Comprehension check
1. Tracey.
2. She's just moved there.
3. Because Tessa is really serious.
4. At the petrol station.
5. She's collecting money for charity.
6. In the town centre.
7. Because she's conscious of the fact that so many people are suffering from poverty in the world.
8. Because he wanted to buy Tessa something really special for Christmas.

9. She thinks that it's a lovely present.
10. Because he's spent all his money on Tessa's present.

Page 36: Language Practice Worksheet 1
1) went (2) was giving (3) got (4) went
(5) were making (6) have earned
(7) fell (8) was collecting (9) collecting
(10) went (11) was going to arrive
(12) had told (13) came (14) said
(15) felt (16) decided
The letters in the grid therefore spell:
blankets and **medicine**.

Page 37: Language Practice Worksheet 2
1. musical 2. designer 3. luckiest
4. petrol station 5. introduce
6. committed 7. generous 8. charity
9. neighbourhood 10. poverty
11. serious.
The word is **millionaire**.

7 The Joke
Page 40: Comprehension check
1. They're sitting on the verandah.
2. She sees some bats.
3. Because bats remind him of ghosts.
4. The ghost visits the house on July the thirteenth, just before eight o'clock.
5. He wears white clothes and a chef's hat.
6. July the thirteenth.
7. Because their uncle has to go to a meeting in the village and their cousin is going out with his girlfriend.
8. Because she's feeling nervous.
9. He's preparing to play a joke on Anna.
10. Because she's really terrified.

Page 42: Language Practice Worksheet 1
a) horror b) nature c) comedy
e) sport f) war film g) children's
h) science fiction
Anna chooses to watch: d) Romance in Rome.

Page 43: Language Practice Worksheet 2
Across: 1. verandah **2.** pancakes
3. towel **4.** gentle **5.** sheet **6.** bat
Down: 1. paradise **2.** ghost
3. garden shed **4.** chef **5.** scary

8 Friendship and Lies
Page 46: Comprehension check
1. Rory wants Lia to go out with him but Lia has schoolwork to do.
2. She has exams soon and she wants to get into university and have a great future.
3. Rory thinks that she should have more fun.

4. Lia says that Rory is being childish.
5. Lia suggests that they meet up in town on Saturday.
6. He plays basketball on Saturday mornings and Friday night is the night for going out.
7. Because the shop assistant will have to go and get the key so there will be no one to see her steal the T-shirts.
8. Seeing Rory and Donna together and seeing Donna shoplifting.
9. Because she had left her purse at home.
10. Because all her money was in the purse.

Page 48: Language Practice Worksheet 1
Exercise 1
The best and most objective introduction is probably the first one, but the choice of introduction depends on the students' own interpretation of the story.
Exercise 2
1) Lia's cousin, Claire; 2) Donna's father;
3) the shop assistant; 4) Lia; 5) Rory;
6) Donna.

Page 49: Language Practice Worksheet 2
Exercise 1
1. left, 2. dropped, 3. torn, 4. forgotten,
5. deleted, 6. stolen, 7. fallen, 8. spilled,
9. blown, 10. given.

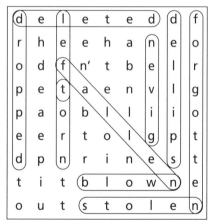

Rory told the English teacher that he had written his essay on the computer but **he hadn't been able to print it out**.
Exercise 2
There are several things which the teacher could say (the first is the most likely):
Find another printer and print it out today.
Give me the essay when your printer is working again.
Print it out on a friend's computer.
Give me the disk and I will read it on-screen.

9 The Concert
Page 52: Comprehension check
1. Because she and Chris haven't quarrelled at all.
2. By going to the cinema.
3. Because so many people wanted to go to the first Micky Farquin concert.
4. She's very excited.
5. He thinks it's a waste of money.
6. She feels upset that Chris won't go to the concert with her.
7. Because it seems disloyal to Chris.
8. She feels that he is selfish.
9. That it's his birthday present.
10. Because he has two tickets for the concert.

Page 54: Language Practice Worksheet 1
1 False, 2 True 3 False, 4 True, 5 False,
6 False, 7 True, 8 False, 9 True,
10 False, 11 False, 12 True, 13 False,
14 False, 15 False, 16 False
The letters spell **Manchester United**.

Page 55: Language Practice Worksheet 2
Exercise 1
1. romantic 2. enthusiastic
3. dismissive 4. disappointed
5. complimentary 6. diplomatic
7. sceptical 8. angry
Exercise 2
1. Can I help you?
2. Yes, have you got any tickets left for the concert?
3. Yes, we've got a few left.
4. How much are the tickets?
5. There are some at £15, and some at £8 left.
6. Are the £8 seats the cheapest?
7. No, there are tickets at £5, but we've sold out of them.
8. OK. I'll take two at £8, please.
9. How would you like to pay?
10. Cash, please.
11. Right. Here are your tickets. Enjoy the show.

10 The Favour
Page 58: Comprehension check
1. She wants to copy parts of his history essays.
2. Because she's too busy to write the essays. She is in the rowing club, she's in the school play and she has a cello exam in a few weeks.
3. She will tell him that they used the same books for research.
4. They are going to visit Emma's grandmother for her birthday.
5. Because she has to go to the regatta on Saturday.
6. She promises that she won't invite more than three friends and no boys.
7. He feels relaxed about it because Emma is very sensible.

8. He wants to tell his parents that he is keeping Emma company that night.
9. Because they'll say he isn't old enough.
10. To find out if she has lied to them about having boys in the house that night.

Page 60: Language Practice Worksheet 1
Each answer will be different, depending on the pupil who is answering the letter.

Page 61: Language Practice Worksheet 2
Exercise 1
1. commiserating 2. agreeing
3. promising 4. advising 5. explaining
6. reassuring 7. hesitating 8. persuading
Exercise 2
Here are some model answers to this exercise, although many different answers may be acceptable.
1. Don't worry. I'll be on time, I promise.
2. Sure. No problem.
3. If I were you, I'd talk to him about how you feel.
4. I can't, I'm afraid. I'm too busy.
5. It sounds like a nightmare.
6. Come on! A good night out will make you feel better.
7. Well, I don't know.
8. Oh, she'll be fine. She's just been very busy recently.

11 Ten-pin Bowling
Page 64: Comprehension check
1. Bowling.
2. The bowling alley isn't in a very nice part of town. The area is a bit rough.
3. He's going to get a taxi home.
4. He's getting a lift with Catherine's dad.
5. He must be home by eleven.
6. Because he has exams soon.
7. Because she's playing a game organised by the youth club against Sonia.
8. They are enemies.
9. He bets £10 that Catherine is going to win.
10. Because Sonia and Russell have stolen the money.

Page 66: Language Practice Worksheet 1
1. No, because I'm going to have an early night.
2. No, because I'm going to the theatre at seven.
3. No, because I'm going to Cascac nightclub at nine.
4. No, because I'm going to go t cinema at nine.
5. No, because I'm going to Anna's party.
6. No, because I have a guitar lesson.
7. No, because I'm going running at six.

8. No, because I'm going to basketball practice at six.
9. No, because I'm going to the theatre on Thursday.
10. No, because I'm going to go to the cinema at nine.
11. No, because I'm going to write my essay.
12. No, because I'm going to visit my grandmother at six.
She can play at seven o'clock on Tuesday or at seven o'clock on Saturday.

Page 67: Language Practice Worksheet 2
Exercise 1
1.b 2.b 3.a 4.a 5.b
Exercise 2

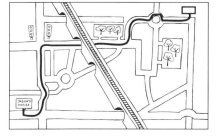

12 The Boy Next Door
Page 70: Comprehension check
1. In her garden.
2. To the town centre and the school.
3. They like the same books and films.
4. Because he's hopeless at sports.
5. Computers and technology.
6. Because he doesn't get invited to things.
7. To the chess club.
8. She really enjoyed it.
9. His party.
10. Because he doesn't like him and thinks he's a nerd (boring person).

Page 72: Language Practice Worksheet 1
Exercise 1
1. Michelle 2. Geoff. 3. Michelle.
4. Dan. 5. Michelle or Dan. 6. Michelle.
7. Michelle. 8. Dan.

Page 73: Language Practice Worksheet 2
Michelle's dad tells her they are moving. (g)
Dan meets Michelle. (b)
Dan offers to show Michelle around town. (f)
Michelle and Dan discuss films and books. (d)
Michelle listens to Dan talking about the robot he's designing at the technology club. (h)
Dan tells Michelle he doesn't get invited to things. (a)
Michelle is invited by Dan to the chess club.(e)
Michelle is invited by Geoff to a party. (c)

Material written by: Jane Myles

Original storylines by: David Evans

Editors: Emma Grisewood and Cheryl Pelteret

Designer: Christine Cox

Cover Photo: Christopher Woods

Cover Design: Kaya Cully

Illustrations by: Nigel Kitching